AFRICAN AMERICAN TRAILBLAZERS

John Lewis

Civil Rights Champion and Congressman

Alison Morretta

Cavendish Square

New York

Published in 2020 by Cavendish Square Publishing, LLC
243 5th Avenue, Suite 136, New York, NY 10016

Copyright © 2020 by Cavendish Square Publishing, LLC

First Edition

Library of Congress Cataloging-in-Publication Data

Names: Morretta, Alison, author.
Title: John Lewis : Civil Rights Champion and Congressman / Alison Morretta.
Description: First edition. | New York, NY : Cavendish Square Publishing, LLC, 2020. |
Series: African American trailblazers | Includes bibliographical references and index. | Audience: Grades 9-12.
Identifiers: LCCN 2018056232 (print) | LCCN 2018057002 (ebook) | ISBN 9781502645500 (ebook) |
ISBN 9781502645494 (library bound) | ISBN 9781502645487 (pbk.)
Subjects: LCSH: Lewis, John, 1940 February 21- | African American civil rights workers--Biography--Juvenile
literature. | Civil rights workers--United States--Biography--Juvenile literature. | United States. Congress.
House--Biography--Juvenile literature. | Legislators--United States--Biography--Juvenile literature.
Classification: LCC E840.8.L43 (ebook) | LCC E840.8.L43 M67 2020 (print) | DDC 328.73/092 [B] --dc23
LC record available at https://lccn.loc.gov/2018056232

Editorial Director: David McNamara
Editor: Kristen Susienka
Copy Editor: Rebecca Rohan
Associate Art Director: Alan Sliwinski
Designer: Joe Parenteau
Production Coordinator: Karol Szymczuk
Photo Research: J8 Media

CONTENTS

A Man of Action

Congressman John Lewis has spent his entire life fighting for civil rights and equality for all Americans. By the time he was in his early twenties, he had done more to bring about substantive change in the United States than most people do in a lifetime. Growing up black in Alabama in the 1940s and 1950s, Lewis learned very quickly that the races were separate, but they were not equal. Even as a teenager, he was determined to do something about that.

Faith in Action

Lewis's faith is incredibly important to him, and he originally wanted to become a minister like his idol, Dr.

On February 14, 2015, Congressman John Lewis stands on the Edmund Pettus Bridge where he and other civil rights activists were met with violent opposition from local authorities nearly fifty years earlier.

Martin Luther King Jr. The social gospel that King preached spoke to Lewis, who ultimately decided to commit to activism full time. He used his time at seminary school in Nashville, Tennessee, to learn and practice the philosophy of nonviolence and lead a student movement that would make headlines. Lewis chose a new career path, but he did not abandon his faith. Instead, he applied it to his work. His form of nonviolent activism was his faith in action.

One of Lewis's most deeply held beliefs is in the Beloved Community about which Dr. King preached so passionately. For Lewis, the Beloved Community is the ultimate life goal; it is true social justice and harmony, only achievable through nonviolent action. According to the King Center, which works to promote the reverend's legacy and ideals, the Beloved Community is "a global vision, in which all people can share in the wealth of the earth." In it, problems such as poverty, hunger, and homelessness aren't tolerated because people simply do not allow it. "Racism and all forms of discrimination, bigotry, and prejudice will be replaced by an all-inclusive spirit of sisterhood and brotherhood." In this community, international disputes are resolved peacefully, rather than through military strength and dominance. "Love and trust will triumph over fear and hatred. Peace with justice will prevail over war and military conflict." The Beloved Community is, for Lewis, nothing short of the kingdom of God on earth.[1]

Lewis has worked toward this goal since he was a teenager, putting his physical safety and freedom on the line over and over. As a young man, he suffered verbal abuse, beatings, and jailing by the enemies of equality in the Jim Crow South, but he never faltered or wavered or resorted to violence in the face of all that hate. From lunch counters in Nashville to bus rides down into the Deep South, voter registration in Mississippi,

Lewis speaks at a 2013 immigration rally at the US Capitol, encouraging Congress to pass immigration reform legislation and to provide a pathway to citizenship for the millions of undocumented immigrants living in the United States.

and a dangerous clash on a bridge in Selma, Alabama, John Lewis has been at the forefront of the civil rights movement, working toward that Beloved Community.

Embracing Politics

Lewis decided to go into politics in order to try to effect change from the inside. He was elected to Congress as the US House Representative for Georgia's Fifth District in 1986 and has held that office ever since. In his position as a congressman, he has always been outspoken when it comes to things he views as unjust, and he votes with his conscience.

Now in his late seventies, Lewis is still out in the streets protesting with the people, leading sit-ins, and even being arrested, all in the name of what he believes is right. He does this not just for black Americans but for the LGBTQ community, immigrants, and other groups being denied their right to freedom and equality. And he will continue to champion for the rights of others for years to come.

CHAPTER ONE

A Difficult History

America has a long history of mistreatment against its black citizens. Even before the country had declared its independence in 1776, there had been a century of bringing African people to colonial America as slaves. These people (and their children, born in the New World) were subject to violence and racial inequalities. Things worsened as the Constitution of the newly independent United States codified the slave system into America's earliest laws.

The economic power of the United States, especially that of the Southern states, was built on slave labor, but slaves were not considered citizens of the country they built. Even the Reconstruction Amendments passed after the Civil War—the Thirteenth, which abolished slavery;

This 1865 illustration depicts former slaves traveling north after their emancipation following the Civil War and the passage of the Thirteenth Amendment, which abolished slavery.

the Fourteenth Amendment, which granted citizenship and equal rights; and the Fifteenth Amendment, which granted voting rights to African American men—were not enough to change things. It would take another century for the United States to pass comprehensive civil rights legislation, and even that was not enough to put an end to the racism so ingrained into many US citizens.

Jim Crow Laws

John Robert Lewis was born in Alabama in 1940, a time when African Americans were subject to racially discriminatory laws meant to keep them subordinate to white Americans. These laws, which had been in place since the failure of Reconstruction, were known as Jim Crow laws. Some of these were actual laws, and others were codes of conduct that black Americans were expected to obey, even though they were not technically legal requirements.

The legal precedent for these laws was the United States Supreme Court's decision in *Plessy v. Ferguson*, established in 1896. In this case, plaintiff Homer Plessy challenged Louisiana's Separate Car Act, which required separate railroad cars and facilities for black and white passengers. On June 7, 1892, Plessy (a mixed-race man) purchased a ticket and boarded the "whites only" car in an attempt to challenge the law. He was arrested when he refused to ride in the "colored" car. The case went to the US Supreme Court, where Plessy's lawyers argued that this law violated the Constitutional rights provided to African Americans under the equal protection clause of the Fourteenth Amendment. The court's 7–1 decision declared that the Fourteenth Amendment only applied to political rights (i.e., the right to vote) but not to social rights, such as shared facilities.

In what became known as the "separate but equal" doctrine, Justice Henry Brown wrote the majority opinion of the court, in which he declared:

> We consider the underlying fallacy of the plaintiff's argument to consist in the assumption that the enforced separation of the two races stamps the colored race with a badge of inferiority. If this be so, it is not by reason of anything found in the act, but solely because the colored race chooses to put that construction upon it ... The argument also assumes that social prejudice may be overcome by legislation, and that equal rights cannot be secured except by an enforced commingling of the two races ... If the civil and political rights of both races be equal, one cannot be inferior to the other civilly or politically. If one race be inferior to the other socially, the Constitution of the United States cannot put them upon the same plane.[1]

This decision legalized segregation based on the idea that segregated facilities would be equal, but this was far from the case. Black facilities were vastly inferior to white facilities. In the wake of the *Plessy* decision, Jim Crow laws began to flourish in the South.

"Jim Crow" was a derogatory term for an African American, made popular by a minstrel play in the mid-nineteenth century, which featured a character with the same name. The Jim Crow laws in Lewis's home state of Alabama were similar to those throughout the South. The state constitution had required separate schools for black and white students since 1875. The jails, too, were segregated; black and white prisoners were not chained together or imprisoned in the same cell. White nurses were not permitted to attend to black male patients. Public facilities like bathrooms and drinking fountains were segregated, as well as railroad cars, ticket windows, waiting areas, and bus seating. Miscegenation (mixed-race marriage) had also been illegal since 1865, but a 1940 state code expanded the law to include cohabitation. The penalty for violating this law was two to seven years in prison, and anyone who performed a mixed-race marriage was subject to a fine of up to $1,000 ($17,600 in 2018) and six months in prison.

Jim Crow Etiquette

In addition to state laws, African Americans were forced to obey Jim Crow etiquette: a set of social rules that black people had to follow in their daily lives and interactions with white people. A black man could not shake hands with a white man because it implied social equality; a black man attempting to shake hands or in any way touch a white woman could be accused of rape. Black people were always introduced to white people (and not the other way around), and white people were to be referred to formally (using mister, missus, miss, sir, ma'am, etc.), while black people were only referred to by their first names. Adult black men were commonly referred to as "boy." Black and white people were not to eat together or in the same location without some sort of separation, and whites were always served first.

In conversation with white people, the following rules applied: do not imply or accuse a white person of lying; never claim superiority to a white person in any area (examples were intelligence and strength); never curse at a white person; never laugh at a white person; never comment on the appearance of a white person, especially a white woman. There were also many other small things, like stepping aside for white people and giving white drivers the right of way. If these social codes of racial etiquette were not followed, a black person could be arrested, injured, or even killed.

Lynching

Racially motivated murders were called lynchings. While it is hard to determine an exact number, a 2015 report by the Equal Justice Initiative puts the number of lynchings of black Americans between 1877 and 1950 at over four thousand. Most of these occurred in the South and Southern border states, but some occurred in Northern urban areas like Detroit and Chicago, as well as scattered incidents in more rural areas of the North. Lynchings were commonly carried out against black men who had been accused of a crime by a white person, especially a black man accused of raping a white woman. Lynching of women was much less common but did occur. Other crimes that carried the threat of lynching included petty theft, labor disputes, assault, arson, and murder. The accused was just that—accused—and didn't even have to be arrested, tried, or convicted of said crime to be viciously punished for it. They were assumed guilty, and in the Jim Crow South that meant they could be executed outside the confines of the law with impunity. Local authorities were often directly involved in these killings.

While the majority of lynchings occurred in the late nineteenth and early twentieth centuries, there were many instances through the mid-twentieth century. These were not the spectacle lynchings of earlier years, where mobs of hundreds would gather to torture and kill the victims in public, but they were just as vicious and deadly.

The Murder of Emmett Till

One lynching had a particularly significant effect on both the emerging civil rights movement and on John Lewis personally. On August 24, 1955, a fourteen-year-old boy named Emmett Till bought some candy from a drugstore in Money, Mississippi.

Sixteen-year-old Emmett Till was the victim of a brutal lynching in Money, Mississippi, in 1955, after being falsely accused of harassment by a white woman.

Of all the Southern states, Mississippi was the most intensely repressive and dangerous for African Americans at the time. Till, who was from Chicago and visiting family, allegedly whistled at and made a comment to a white woman on his way out of the store. The woman was twenty-one-year-old Caroline Bryant, and her husband, Roy Bryant, was the store's owner.

Several days later, on the night of August 28, Roy Bryant and his half-brother J.W. Milam kidnapped Emmett Till at gunpoint from his great-uncle's home, beat him, and shot him in the head before disposing of him by tying a cotton gin fan to his body with barbed wire and throwing him in the Tallahatchie River. His bloated, disfigured corpse was found three days later. Bryant and Milam were charged with Till's murder but were acquitted by an all-white, all-male jury. Knowing they could not be convicted of the crime because of the law of double jeopardy—in which you cannot be tried twice for the same crime—Bryant and Milam admitted to murdering Till in an interview with *Look* magazine in January 1956.

Though it had long been assumed that Caroline Bryant lied, it was confirmed in 2017. Bryant (now Caroline Donham) admitted that she lied about Till's actions in an interview with Duke University professor Timothy B. Tyson for his 2017 book *The Blood of Emmett Till*. She claims she does not remember exactly what happened in the store but that Till did not, as she testified in court, physically grab her or sexually harass her in any way. The Emmett Till Unsolved Civil Rights Crime Act—which was sponsored by Congressman John Lewis—was passed in 2008; in 2016, it was updated to expand its scope and strengthen the requirements of the Justice Department. This act is not just about Till but about solving many of the racially motivated unsolved murders of the pre-civil rights era. Till's case in particular was reopened in July 2018. As of late 2018, no charges had been pressed against Caroline Bryant Donham, who was in her eighties.

The Emmett Till murder made national news at a time when the organized civil rights movement was just beginning and was a galvanizing force for many people. Emmett's mother, Mamie, insisted on having an open-coffin funeral that was open to the public. She wanted everyone to see the gruesome reality of what had happened to her son. Tens of thousands of people attended the Chicago funeral, including reporters from *Jet* magazine. Mamie Till allowed them to photograph her son's disfigured corpse, and they published the explicit photos in their September 15, 1955, issue. People all across America saw the photos of what happened to Till in Mississippi, and the fact that Bryant and Milam were acquitted struck many as a blatant miscarriage of justice.

John Lewis was only a year older than Till at the time of the murder, and he was "shaken to the core" by it. In his autobiography, *Walking With the Wind*, Lewis writes, "I was fifteen, black, at the edge of my own manhood, just like him. He could have been me … It had been only a year since I was so elated at the *Brown* decision. Now I felt like a fool. It didn't seem that the Supreme Court mattered. It didn't seem that the American principles of justice and equality I read about in my beat-up civics book at school mattered."[2] As dejected as Lewis was by the murder of Till, within a few months he would be energized by a mass movement happening in his home state of Alabama.

The Montgomery Bus Boycott

The single most influential event in John Lewis's youth was the Montgomery bus boycott: a coordinated, yearlong campaign of direct-action civil disobedience in Montgomery,

THE *BROWN* DECISION

The National Association for the Advancement of Colored People (NAACP), a civil rights organization founded in 1909 with the mission of eliminating racial discrimination and ensuring equal rights for all citizens, looked to the federal court system to fight the segregation legitimized by the *Plessy* decision. Lawyer Thurgood Marshall, who would later serve as the first black Supreme Court justice, was chief counsel for the NAACP and argued the case of *Brown v. Board of Education of Topeka* in front of the court. On May 17, 1954, the court issued its unanimous 9–0 opinion that segregation of public schools was unconstitutional. Chief Justice Earl Warren wrote the opinion of the court, in which he stated: "segregation of children in public schools solely on the basis of race deprives children of the minority group of equal educational opportunities." He went on to say that "in the field of public education, the doctrine of 'separate but equal' has no place. Separate educational facilities are inherently unequal."[3]

The *Brown* decision initially gave hope to the African American people living under Jim Crow, but it had no real immediate effect except sparking backlash from white Southerners who were extremely against integration. White Citizens' Councils (WCC)—whose membership included influential businessmen, local law enforcement, and government officials—formed across the South. These white supremacist organizations used economic and social intimidation tactics to oppress African Americans as well as white people who supported integration. Tactics included loss of employment and housing, business boycotts, and voter suppression.

A group of African American men in Montgomery, Alabama, walk to work instead of using public transportation. This was during the 381-day boycott to desegregate city buses—an event that inspired young John Lewis to become an activist.

Alabama. Long before Rosa Parks refused to give up her seat on a Montgomery bus, there were plans for a boycott there. Jo Ann Robinson, president of the Women's Political Council (WPC), had planned to boycott the city buses in response to the unjust treatment that she and so many other black women in Montgomery routinely suffered on the bus. In May 1954, Robinson sent Montgomery mayor William A. Gayle a letter of demands. This letter did not call for full desegregation but for more equal treatment, including more bus stops in black communities and the right to enter at the front of the bus instead of purchasing a ticket at the front and being forced to enter in the rear. Robinson threatened a boycott if demands were not met, but the city took no action. The boycott did not take place, but Robinson's planning was instrumental in the success of the boycott the following year.

On December 1, 1955, Rosa Parks famously refused to give up her seat on the bus for a white man. A common misconception about Parks is that she was just an average seamstress, too tired to move. The reality of the situation is that Parks was tired of giving in. She had been secretary of the local branch of the NAACP for over a decade before the boycott, working alongside E.D. Nixon, president of the NAACP's Alabama state branch.

Parks was arrested but quickly bailed out by Nixon. When Jo Ann Robinson received news of the arrest, she quickly put in place a plan to execute a citywide bus boycott. She worked through the night making copies of a notice to be distributed throughout the black community, calling for everyone to stay off the buses the coming Monday, December 5. Meanwhile, Nixon was looking to local ministers for support. At this time, Dr. Martin Luther King Jr. was a young pastor who was new in town. King agreed to let Nixon use the Dexter Avenue Baptist Church for a meeting to organize the boycott. At a meeting held on December 2, King was elected president of the newly formed Montgomery Improvement Association (MIA) that would lead the boycott.

The boycott lasted over a year, with the black citizens of Montgomery walking and using an organized ride-sharing system. All attempts to negotiate with city officials were met with resistance, and the boycott brought outright hostility from the white community. Membership in the Montgomery White Citizens' Council soared and included members of local government and law enforcement. The local Ku Klux Klan (KKK), a white supremacist organization, also became involved, both in intimidating and perpetrating acts of domestic terrorism against local leaders. The houses of King and Nixon were firebombed, and boycotters were subject to harassment and physical attacks. In February 1956, seventy-five boycott leaders (including Parks and King) were arrested and charged with violating a 1921 Alabama state law against boycotting without just cause (although only King's case went to trial and his conviction was overturned on appeal).

The NAACP decided that Parks's was not the ideal test case to challenge the bus segregation laws in the courts. Instead, they filed a class action lawsuit against the city of Montgomery, with Mayor Gayle as the defendant. The plaintiffs—Aurelia Browder, Claudette Colvin, Susie McDonald, and Mary Louise Smith—were all black women who had been arrested for violating Montgomery bus segregation laws. They filed in the US District Court of Alabama, which ruled 2–1 that bus segregation violated the Fourteenth Amendment rights to equal protection. The city and state appealed, and the case went to the Supreme Court. In *Browder v. Gayle* (1956), the Supreme Court upheld the district court's verdict and ordered the state of Alabama to desegregate its buses.

The buses were desegregated on December 21, 1956—381 days after the boycott began—but that did not put an end to the violence in Montgomery. There was a drive-by shooting at King's home, white citizens shot at city buses and attacked riders at bus stops, and bombings at homes and churches continued. There was also still segregation of public facilities and at establishments like restaurants and department stores. While the bus boycott did not put an end to all segregation, it inspired many black Americans and proved that activism through nonviolent protest could bring about tangible results.

Dr. Martin Luther King Jr. was a mentor and friend to John Lewis. The two men worked closely together to effect change during the civil rights movement of the 1960s.

John Lewis credits the Montgomery bus boycott for changing his life:

> More than any other event before or since … This wasn't just talk. This was action. And it was a different kind of action from anything I'd heard of before. This was a fight, but it was a different way of fighting. It wasn't about confrontation or violence. Those 50,000 black men and women in Montgomery were using their will and their dignity to take a stand, to resist. They weren't responding with their fists; they were speaking with their feet.[4]

Seeing King's role in the boycotts made Lewis more committed than ever to become a minister, because it showed him that one could be a minister and use that role to promote social justice through Christian principles.

Voter Disenfranchisement

Technically, all African Americans had the right to vote by 1920, when the Nineteenth Amendment gave voting rights to women (African American men were given the vote in the Fifteenth Amendment). In reality, in the later twentieth century, black Americans were overwhelmingly denied voting rights. The white establishment in the South especially feared losing power and political influence if black citizens were allowed to vote. They found ways—both legal and extralegal—to stop them. Some of the legal tactics were to require literacy tests, annual poll taxes, and employment requirements. These laws specifically targeted black voters, many of whom could not read, write, or afford to pay. They also made voter registration difficult, with very limited areas and times made available for new registrants. People who lived in rural communities and made their living farming (a large percentage of the South's black population) could not make the trip; registrars often set times for planting season to make sure that many black farmers could not register. Another tactic was to require a street address when many rural black neighborhoods did not have street names or numbers. Even if by chance a black man or woman was able to meet their state's requirements, it was still at the discretion of white registrars, government employees who oversee voter registration, who would often deny them, either on a technicality or just because they could.

Far more sinister than the legal tactics were the extralegal ones, based on intimidation and violence. Campaigns of terror against black voters had been employed by the KKK since its original formation after the Civil War. The Klan of the 1950s, which had direct ties to local law enforcement and the Southern Democrats, targeted civil rights leaders and activists with bombing campaigns, cross burnings, mob violence, and murder. The threat of unchecked violence was enough to keep many African Americans from attempting to vote. All these factors combined resulted in low voter turnout from black Americans in the South and the subsequent lack of political power and representation in government.

CHAPTER TWO

The Boy from Troy

O n February 21, 1940, John Robert Lewis was born in Troy, Alabama, in the heart of the Jim Crow South. He was the third of ten children born to Eddie and Willie Mae Carter Lewis, who worked as sharecroppers on a farm in rural Pike County. Sharecropping is a type of farming where farmers rented land (and often other equipment and seed) in exchange for a portion, or share, of their crop. Under this system, the landowner made most of the profit without doing most of the work. Like most farms in this region of the United States, the main cash crop was cotton, and young Lewis and all his siblings were expected to help with the backbreaking labor that came with cotton farming. This was difficult work and not profitable under

A sharecropping family, much like Lewis's own, works a cotton field in Alabama in the 1940s.

the sharecropping system—a fact that did not escape the attention of the astute young Lewis.

By the time he was six years old, Lewis understood that there was no way to get ahead in sharecropping. He wrote, "I hated picking cotton … I hated the work itself, but even more than that, from a very early age I realized and resented what it represented: exploitation, hopelessness, a dead-end way of life."[1] He saw his hardworking parents mired in debt, having to hand over half of their crop to the Copeland family, with whom they had their arrangement. After taking the first half, the Copelands would then subtract from the other half what the Lewises owed for supplies such as seed, fertilizer, and farming equipment. What was left belonged to the Lewises, but it was never enough.

Preaching to the Chickens

From a young age, Lewis knew that he wanted to be a preacher. The Christian faith was a huge part of his life growing up, and his parents were very religious. The Lewis home did not have electricity or running water, but they did have a battery-powered radio, and every Sunday they would tune to the local gospel station, WRMA. The Bible was one of the few reading materials available in the Lewis household.

In the rural area where the Lewises lived, the roads were not paved, and it was difficult to make it to church regularly. In addition to the journey there, there was so much work to do on the farm that it was not feasible for the Lewises and other families in the area to get to church frequently. The area churches—Dunn's Chapel and Macedonia Baptist—held services once a month (on different Sundays), and the Lewises attended both.

For Lewis, attending church services was a joy and an inspiration. It was more than just a religious service; it was a community event. It was a happy occasion for the hardworking people of the area who did not have much contact with others in the community. Church was "a time of congregation … You could feel the energy in the air as people arrived from all directions and gathered in groups outside the church building, everyone talking and laughing and hugging, just getting together."[2] The services were not the end of the festivities, though. Afterward, the Lewises would gather at the home of a relative (usually Lewis's grandfather's house) to socialize.

One of the most well-known anecdotes from Lewis's childhood is how, after his parents put him in charge of the family's chicken coop, he would preach to the chickens. Tending the chickens taught young John Lewis discipline, responsibility, and patience, but it also taught him to have kinship with and compassion for other living creatures. This was not necessarily helpful, since some of the chickens were destined to end up on his dinner table. He would hold funerals for the chickens and give eulogies. He would imagine the chickens as his congregation, reciting to them the Bible verses he learned in Sunday school. He even performed baptisms on some of them. As a result, his family started calling him "preacher."

Education

Like many black children at that time, Lewis's educational opportunities were limited. The elementary school for black students was at the church a half-mile (0.8 kilometers) from where he lived, but there were no buses for black students, so he and the other students walked to Dunn's Chapel Elementary. The two-room schoolhouse was a rundown wooden shack that

As a child, Lewis attended a segregated school such as this one. School segregation resulted in educational disparities between white and black children, with facilities for black children vastly inferior to those for whites.

had no water or well, and no electricity or heat. In addition to their schoolwork, the children were responsible for gathering wood and water. There was one teacher for all the grades, around seventy students total, and the school received no government funding, except for the teacher's salary. Everything else they needed was provided via funds raised by the community.

Young Lewis loved to read, and through books he was able to learn about the world outside his rural community. He especially enjoyed reading biographies of influential African Americans such as Booker T. Washington and George Washington Carver.

After elementary school, Lewis's only option was the black junior high school several miles away. There was a bus service to take students to the school, but the buses were old and the roads unpaved and treacherous in bad weather—until they reached the white area, which was paved. Every time he rode the bus, Lewis went past the white school, which was modern and well kept and even had a nice playground outside. He also saw the brand-new buses for the white children.

Once he got to school, he thrived. The junior high was larger and better equipped than his elementary school, with multiple classrooms and teachers. Lewis was very committed to his education, which he knew was the key to bettering himself.

Separate but Not Equal

Lewis's parents understood the importance of education, but as with so many black families, work had to come first. The children were needed during farming season, so Lewis and his classmates had to miss a lot of school in order to help out. Young Lewis resented this, especially when he learned that this was not the case for white children.

Though he was not really exposed to white people as a child, as Lewis got older he began to learn things about them from his parents. In addition to farm labor, Willie Mae worked in Troy, cooking and cleaning for white people. She spoke vague warnings to her son about interacting with them. She warned him not to get out of line with white people and not to get in their way, that there were things a person could not do or say around them. Lewis did not fully understand what she meant by this until he went to the nearby town of Troy and experienced racial inequality firsthand.

Lewis first traveled to Troy's main town when he was eight years old. The experience of its segregated facilities had a strong impact on young Lewis. Troy was much the same as any town in the segregated South. There were separate bathrooms and drinking fountains, with facilities for black people less well kept and dirtier than those for white people. At Byrd's drugstore, for instance, black people could purchase whatever they wanted, for the same amount of money as white customers, but they could not sit at the tables or the counter; the black area was a wooden bench outside the store.

Of all the inequalities he saw, the one that bothered Lewis the most was the library, which was not open to black citizens. In his autobiography, he expresses his displeasure with his lack of access to "the public library, where I longed to go, but through whose doors I was not allowed to set foot. That killed me, the idea that this was a *public* library, paid for with government money, and I was supposedly a US citizen, but I wasn't allowed in. Even an eight-year-old could see there was something terribly wrong about that."[3] For Lewis, who loved to read, this was the most painful injustice of them all, and it would later inspire his first act of defiance.

In 1956, Lewis approached the librarian at the Pike County Public Library and tried to apply for a library card. He knew he would be refused, but he was committed to performing his first formal act of protest. After being denied, he wrote a petition that the library must be accessible to black people, who paid taxes just like white people, and even passed it around at school for signatures. He didn't get many but mailed it anyway. While he received no response and nothing came of it, it was still a significant moment in his life: "it was a start. It was an *act*, and that meant something, at least to me."[4]

Higher Learning

After junior high, Lewis attended the Pike County Training School (PCTS). There was no high school for black children, and training schools were really just preparing the students for life as farmers or domestic workers. Especially bright students could aspire to become teachers, but this was not the life Lewis wanted. His dream was to be a preacher, and he wanted to pursue that outside of Pike County.

The PCTS library was the first place Lewis had access to black newspapers and magazines, and he was encouraged by the school librarian to read everything he could get his hands on. It was in one of these papers that he first read about the *Brown* decision. Of that experience, Lewis wrote, "I remember the feeling of jubilation I had reading the newspaper story … Everything was going to change now. No longer would I have to ride a broken-down bus almost forty miles [64 km] each day to attend classes at a 'training' school with hand-me-down books and supplies."[5] Unfortunately, nothing actually changed for John Lewis or the black students in the South.

Lewis was the first person in his family to graduate from secondary school and go to college. He was accepted to the American Baptist Theological Seminary (ABT) and began his studies in the fall of 1957. At seminary, he was exposed to philosophical and theological teachings that reinforced his belief in the social gospel—a form of Christianity that applied the teachings of the Bible to social justice issues. Lewis had first been exposed to the social gospel in 1955. This moment was also the first time he heard Dr. Martin Luther King Jr. speak.

He was listening to the radio with his family when he heard King give a sermon called "Paul's Letter to the American Christians." In it, King spoke of applying Christian principles to the issues facing the black community, and how black Christians' focus should be less on reaching the Promised Land and more on solving the problems facing them on earth. Lewis remembers the experience vividly: "his message ... sat me bolt upright with amazement ... I was on fire with the words I was hearing. I felt that this man ... was speaking directly to me."[6] Indeed, King's sermon struck a chord with young Lewis, who was becoming more and more aware of the racial injustices facing black Americans. He did not know it at the time, but the man he was listening to would become his mentor, his friend, and his partner in the civil rights struggles to come.

An Act of Defiance

During Lewis's freshman year at ABT, he was well aware of a school desegregation crisis in Little Rock, Arkansas. The NAACP was testing the *Brown* decision by enrolling nine black students at the previously all-white Central High School. This met with a great deal of resistance, and the bravery of the

During his time at seminary school, Lewis closely followed the story of the Little Rock Nine, a group of African American students attempting to desegregate Central High School in Little Rock, Arkansas, after the *Brown v. Board* decision.

students (called the Little Rock Nine) and the activism of the NAACP inspired Lewis to attempt to form an on-campus NAACP chapter at American Baptist. When the school denied his request, Lewis decided to apply to Troy State University, which did not accept black students.

Lewis applied to Troy State during his Christmas break in 1957 but received no reply. He decided to write a letter to his idol, Dr. King, in which he introduced himself and explained his situation regarding the Troy State application. Lewis received a response from Fred Gray, the civil rights lawyer and activist who had represented Rosa Parks. Gray wrote on King's behalf, asking for more details about Lewis's Troy State application. Lewis was also in contact with Reverend Ralph Abernathy, who had led the bus boycott alongside King. After weeks of correspondence, Gray and Abernathy told Lewis that Dr. King wanted to meet him. They set a date for summer 1957.

When Lewis first met Dr. King in person, King asked him, "Are you the boy from Troy?" At their meeting, Lewis spoke with King, Gray, and Abernathy, who tried to determine Lewis's level of commitment to desegregating Troy State. Lewis recalls that Dr. King was concerned not just for him but for his family. King warned Lewis that his parents could lose their jobs, have their house and farm destroyed, or be assaulted if he chose to go through with it, but Lewis was committed and King agreed to help him. All he needed was permission from his parents.

While his mother and father were proud of him and initially supported him, they were very afraid of what could happen. In the end, Lewis's parents did not give permission. He was disappointed but understood that the risk was too great for them.

Learning Nonviolence

During his second year at ABT, Lewis attended church services every Sunday at First Colored Baptist Church. There, he listened to sermons by Reverend Kelly Miller Smith. One Sunday in September, Reverend Smith announced that James Lawson of the Fellowship of Reconciliation (FOR) would be holding a workshop that evening, and Lewis decided to attend. Lewis was aware of FOR because they had published an illustrated pamphlet about the Montgomery bus boycott that explained

JAMES LAWSON

One of the most important figures in Lewis's life was Reverend James Lawson, who taught him the practical application of nonviolent civil disobedience. Lawson was a conscientious objector during the Korean War and served time in prison.

After his release, he went to teach in India and studied the nonviolent philosophy of Mahatma Gandhi. Gandhi's commitment to nonviolent civil disobedience—both in the struggle for equality for Indians in South Africa

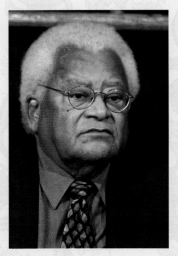

Civil rights leader James Lawson in 2011

and for India's independence from British rule—inspired Lawson, who saw how these principles could be applied to the US civil rights movement. Lawson saw firsthand how the Indian caste system and colonial oppression in the 1940s was similar to the racial segregation and civil rights violations occurring in the United States in the 1950s and 1960s.

Lawson moved to Nashville, Tennessee, in 1958 and became field secretary for the pacifist organization Fellowship of Reconciliation (FOR). It was at a FOR meeting that Lewis first heard Lawson speak and was instantly drawn to him and his teachings. Lawson led workshops that taught students

tactics for nonviolent resistance. His teachings and organization were crucial to the success of the Nashville student movement and sit-ins. He was also active in the Student Nonviolent Coordinating Committee (SNCC) and wrote that organization's founding statement. Lewis worked closely with Lawson when he was a student activist, and Lawson's teachings formed the basis for Lewis's philosophy and the method of activism he would apply throughout his life.

the principles of nonviolent direct action. At the first meeting, Lawson spoke generally about how all the major world religions shared one basic tenet—the concept of justice—and that he would be holding workshops every Tuesday night on this topic.

Lewis began attending these workshops every Tuesday. Lawson taught students the philosophy of nonviolence, which at its essence is the capacity for love and forgiveness—the social gospel in action. Lawson's workshops also taught students the practical application of nonviolence in the face of hostility. Students would act out different scenarios they would encounter at a protest—both verbal and physical attacks—with some students playing the role of protestor and others the antagonist.

Lawson taught them how to position their bodies to protect internal organs during a beating, and how to help others by putting their own body in the way to minimize damage. They also learned the importance of maintaining eye contact with an attacker as a way of disarming them. Students acted out sit-ins and practiced nonviolent reactions to being yelled, cursed at, pushed, and shoved. Most importantly, Lawson taught the students that "it was not enough … simply to endure a beating. It was not enough to resist the urge to strike back at an assailant. That urge can't *be* there … You have to do more than just not hit back. You have to have no *desire* to hit back. You have to *love* that person who's hitting you."[7] The concept of loving someone in the face of hatred and violence is a lesson that shaped Lewis's life's work.

Lawson was integral to the formal organization of the Nashville student movement, which was made up of students from the area's four historical black colleges and universities (HBCUs): ABT, Fisk University, Meharry Medical College, and Tennessee Agricultural and Industrial (now Tennessee State University). Students from these institutions flocked to

Lawson's workshops, where they prepared for a direct-action campaign targeting segregated facilities in Nashville.

The Nashville Sit-Ins

By October 1959, the Nashville student movement was formally organized and had decided on the target of their first direct-action campaign. Lawson had spent time speaking to members of the community and heard overwhelmingly from the black women of Nashville that they were most bothered by segregation at downtown department stores. They felt insulted and humiliated by the experience of shopping alongside white women, spending the same money, but not being allowed to try on clothing or sit at the lunch counters.

On Saturday morning, November 28, 1959, Lewis and other members of the student movement staged their first sit-in at a downtown department store called Harvey's. They intended to purchase something and then, once they established themselves as paying customers, sit down at the lunch counter to have a meal. As expected, the waitress told them they could not be served. At this point, group member Diane Nash—who was the appointed speaker for the sit-in, since part of the plan was that one person was to speak for everyone—asked to speak to the manager. The manager also denied her, stating that the store's policy was not to serve black customers. Nash then asked if the white members of their group could be served, and the manager said they would not be served because they were there with the black students. Nash thanked the manager, and the group left without incident.

This first sit-in was a trial run for many more to come. January 1960 was filled with planning and organizing the coming campaign, but on February 1, a group of black college students in Greensboro, North Carolina, staged a sit-in at a Woolworth's counter. These four freshmen from North Carolina Agricultural and Technical State University—Ezell Blair Jr., Franklin McCain, David Richmond, and Joseph McNeil—had nothing to do with the Nashville movement, but they had the same experience of discrimination. This drove them to stage their own sit-in protest, and over the next few days, more and more local students joined them.

The Greensboro sit-ins garnered national attention, and while not the first action of its type, they were the sparks that set off the direct action sit-in movement that Lewis and the other members of the Nashville student movement had been working toward.

The sit-ins, which were occurring in cities throughout the segregated South, started making national news, and the Nashville group sprung to action. The first citywide sit-in, coordinated by the Nashville student movement and the Nashville Christian Leadership Council, was planned for February 13. That day 124 students participated in lunchtime sit-ins at stores throughout the city. They went in groups of around twenty-five people, black and white, to lunch counters throughout the city's downtown area.

Lewis was a part of the group that went to Woolworth's. He was his group's designated speaker that day and asked the waitress if they could be served. She responded in the negative (and used a racial slur). The other customers left, and soon one of the waitresses came out of the back with a handwritten sign that said "COUNTER CLOSED." The lights were turned off, and the waitresses left, leaving Lewis and his group alone in the dark. They stayed for several hours, studying quietly. At one point, they were taunted by young white men, but otherwise it was uneventful.

The second Nashville sit-in occurred on February 18. This time, it was over two hundred students strong. Lewis was part of a group that went to W.T. Grant's department store, and it went the same way as the first: they were refused service, the counter was closed, and they stayed a few hours without major incident. On February 20, over three hundred students participated in a campaign that now included the local Walgreens. At this point, the stores began to take action against the protestors, stacking goods on top of counters so that the students could not study as they sat there. People inside the store would taunt the students. Outside, angry crowds complained to reporters, who were taking notice of the events, that they could not eat at the counters.

That evening, storeowners called on the activists to suspend their protests until an agreement could be reached. They agreed to wait, but a week went by without any response. They planned another campaign for Saturday, February 27. The day before, the chief of police in Nashville sent word to the group that anyone protesting would be arrested for disorderly conduct and trespassing. The students were also concerned by rumors, communicated to them by a white minister sympathetic to their cause, that a group of young white men planned to attack the protestors with no interference from the police.

Since the movement had grown very large very quickly, many protestors did not have the same training that Lewis, Nash, and the original members had received from Lawson. To avoid unnecessary problems, Lewis wrote a list of guidelines, which were distributed to protestors ahead of the Saturday sit-ins. This list came to be known as the Nashville Student Code:

DO NOT: 1. Strike back nor curse if abused.
2. Laugh out.
3. Hold conversations with floor walker.

4. Leave your seat until your leader has given you permission to do so.
5. Block entrances to stores outside nor the aisles inside.

DO: 1. Show yourself friendly and courteous at all times.
2. Sit straight; always face the counter.
3. Report all serious incidents to your leader.
4. Refer information seekers to your leader in a polite manner.
5. Remember the teachings of Jesus Christ, Mahatma Gandhi, and Martin Luther King. Love and nonviolence is the way.[8]

As expected, the February 27 sit-ins were met with violence. Lewis was part of the group sitting in at Woolworth's, and before they even got there, they were harassed on the street by white teenagers who pushed and shoved them as they walked downtown. Once inside the store, they were accosted by white men shouting racial slurs and trying to goad them into a physical fight. They resisted, drawing on their training and philosophy of nonviolence, but this only made the white mob angrier.

Lewis and other members of the Woolworth's group were attacked; Lewis was hit in the ribs and watched as a man stubbed out a lit cigarette on one of the other protestors. Despite these events, the protestors followed the plan, returning to their seats and sitting quietly even when under attack.

Woolworth's wasn't the only violent scene that day. At another store, Kress's, protestors were sprayed with mustard and ketchup. There were reporters on the scene at the McClellan's

Two women sit at a Nashville, Tennessee, lunch counter in protest of the city's segregated public facilities during student sit-in campaigns of 1960. John Lewis was one of the main organizers and participants.

store too. There, television cameras filmed as one of the white students, Paul LaPrad, was viciously beaten. The footage aired that evening on the national news, bringing the reality of the situation into homes across America.

When the police arrived, it was not to arrest the white mob but their victims: the student protestors. Lewis, along with nearly one hundred other protestors, was arrested for disorderly conduct. This, his first arrest, was one of the most significant moments in his life. He writes:

> I felt no shame or disgrace. I didn't feel fear, either
> ... I felt exhilarated ... [The police van] seemed
> like a chariot to me, a freedom vehicle carrying me

across a threshold. I had wondered all along … how I would handle the reality of what I had studied and trained and prepared for for so long, what it would be like to actually face pain and rage and the power of uniformed authority. Now I knew. Now I had crossed over, I had stepped through the door into total, unquestioning commitment.[9]

As part of their protest, Lewis and the others did not accept bail money. This "jail no bail" strategy was a part of their protest.

This was Lewis's first arrest, but it would not be his last. Over the years, he would be arrested forty-five times. Most recently, at age seventy-three, Lewis participated in a sit-in outside the US Capitol Building in Washington, DC, at a 2013 rally for immigration reform. He was arrested for his act of civil disobedience, proving that his early life's dedication to direct action would not wane during his political career. He would always believe in fighting for equality and human rights in the face of oppression, not just for black Americans but for anyone being treated unjustly.

Lewis saw his first success on May 10, 1960, when the six downtown stores he and his fellow protestors had targeted served food to black customers at their lunch counters for the first time. The sit-ins taught John Lewis a powerful lesson he would carry with him throughout his life: that everyday citizens committed to nonviolent direct action can and will effect change.

CHAPTER THREE

Different Visions for Change

Lewis's involvement in the Southern freedom campaigns of the early 1960s made him one of the most visible leaders in the youth-led civil rights movement. As such, he worked closely with many other civil rights organizations and influential people. As a leader of the Student Nonviolent Coordinating Committee (SNCC, pronounced "snick") and board member of the Southern Christian Leadership Conference (SCLC), he formed relationships with the nation's most influential civil rights leaders. Some of these relationships were contentious, as not everyone shared Lewis's specific vision for effecting change on a national level. As time went on and SNCC grew larger, Lewis would even find himself at odds with members of his own organization.

Dr. Martin Luther King Jr. (*first from left, first row*) leads the March on Washington for Jobs and Freedom on August 28, 1963.

SCLC and the Formation of SNCC

The Southern Christian Leadership Conference (SCLC) was formed in 1957 after the Montgomery bus boycott, with Martin Luther King Jr. as its president. The goal of the organization was to promote civil equality through nonviolent means. The SCLC was closely tied to the African American churches in the South, since the church was at the heart of many black communities. Most SCLC leaders were ministers who used the pulpit and the organized church community as a way to spread their vision of social justice.

On Easter weekend 1960, SCLC executive secretary Ella Baker organized a conference at Shaw University in Raleigh, North Carolina. This conference would see over two hundred black college students in attendance. During this gathering, SNCC was formally begun. Dr. King's initial goal for this meeting was to harness the energy of the student movement and bring the students into the SCLC fold, but Ella Baker disagreed with this strategy. She understood that the students valued their autonomy and that they were better off forming a separate, independent organization with guidance and support from older leaders. While Lewis did not attend the conference—he stayed in Nashville to organize sit-ins—James Lawson, Diane Nash, and others represented the Nashville group there.

While SNCC was explicitly formed as a nonviolent direct-action organization, from the very beginning there were some members who were not fully committed to nonviolence in the same way the Nashville group was. People who did not have Lawson's extensive training did not fully grasp the idea of total nonviolence and love in the face of hate that Lewis, Nash, and the others had been trained on. Among the most prominent early SNCC members who did not subscribe to the philosophy of nonviolence were Stokely Carmichael and James Forman, both of whom would hold leadership positions in the organization and clash with Lewis. Carmichael, Forman, and others were not pro-violence, but they did believe in self-defense and questioned the commitment to nonviolence and the spirit of redemptive love that Lewis and other members of the Nashville group had learned from Lawson. This would become one of many significant divisions among SNCC's leadership in later years, but it was there from the beginning.

The organization was also divided over the focus it should take—continuing direct-action campaigns or shifting focus to voter registration. Veterans of the Nashville movement like Lewis, Diane Nash, and James Bevel were adamant that they continue the direct-action campaigns that had proved successful, but others believed that voter registration would be a more effective use of resources. In 1961, after the Freedom Rides campaign to desegregate bus facilities in the South brought racial violence to the attention of the nation, the Kennedy administration had urged the movement to shift its focus away from desegregation to voting rights, even offering funding for the latter. This was in many ways a self-serving move because more black voters would mean more votes for John F. Kennedy, whereas more demonstrations meant continued unrest and bad publicity, as well as loss of Southern Democratic support. Founding members of SNCC, especially Lewis and Nash, wanted to stick to their roots and continue to focus on nonviolent direct action against segregation. However, it would soon become clear that both direct-action and voter registration were equally important to the civil rights movement, and so two wings of SNCC were formed to address both strategies.

President Kennedy's Address

Lewis was elected chairman of SNCC in June 1963 and moved to Atlanta, Georgia, where SNCC's headquarters were located. That same month, President Kennedy gave his famous "Address on Civil Rights" to the nation. The address was a direct response to the televised violence that had erupted in Birmingham, Alabama, during April and May of that year; it was also a response to Southern segregationists' attempts to block admission of black students to a Mississippi school in 1962 and an Alabama school in 1963. Both times, Kennedy was forced to send in the National Guard to protect the black students and force local authorities to integrate the schools.

President Kennedy's televised address on June 11, 1963, called for the nation to acknowledge that the American promise of equality and freedom for all was not being honored for its black citizens. He noted:

> The nation was founded ... on the principle that all men are created equal, and that the rights of every man are diminished when the rights of one man are threatened ... It ought to be possible, therefore, for American students of any color to attend any public institution they select without having to be backed up by troops. It ought to be possible for American consumers of any color to receive equal service in places of public accommodation, such as hotels and restaurants, and theaters and retail stores without being forced to resort to demonstrations on the street.

This address was a call to action, not only for the average American to "examine his conscience" but also for legislators to pass his proposed civil rights bill.[1]

The "Big Six"

Kennedy's speech came at a time when a group of civil rights leaders (later known as the "Big Six") were planning a mass march on Washington, DC. The six men organizing the march were A. Philip Randolph, Martin Luther King Jr. of SCLC, Roy Wilkins of the NAACP, Whitney Young of the National Urban League, James Farmer of the Congress of Racial Equality (CORE), and John Lewis of SNCC. The Kennedy administration did not want it to go forward, however, and called for a meeting with the movement leaders to try to dissuade them. Kennedy believed that the march would have

President John F. Kennedy (*front, third from right*) meets with the Big Six organizers and other march participants in the Oval Office. Lewis (*partially obscured*) can be seen behind and to the right of Dr. Martin Luther King (*second from left*).

a negative effect on his chance to pass a civil rights bill. Lewis recalls Kennedy saying, "We want success in Congress ... not just a big show at the Capitol" and that the "bill stood a much better chance of passing if black people stayed off the streets."[2] However, the Big Six were insistent that the march would take place despite Kennedy's reservations.

Among this group of important men, Randolph was the undisputed leader of the 1963 march initiative, and all the men, including John Lewis, had a great deal of respect and admiration for him. Randolph had been an activist since the early 1900s. In 1925, he organized the Brotherhood of Sleeping Car Porters to help black workers unionize and receive equal treatment. During World War II, Randolph's focus shifted to fighting segregation in the military and defense industries. His first proposed March on Washington occurred in 1941, and this threat of demonstration led directly to President Franklin D. Roosevelt issuing an executive order that banned racial discrimination in the defense industry.

Dr. King represented the SCLC in the Big Six. As the most visible and well-known civil rights leader in 1963, his presence and participation were essential to the success of the march, but he was not in charge of the planning. That was left to Randolph and Bayard Rustin, another long-time activist who was not part of the Big Six but whose behind-the-scenes planning was crucial to the event's success. King and the SCLC agreed with Randolph regarding the purpose of the march, which was initially about employment. Eventually, however, it evolved and expanded to include both economic disparity and the general civil rights violations suffered by African Americans. While Lewis and King did not always agree on strategy, Lewis had a great love and respect for King and considered him a mentor and a friend.

Roy Wilkins was the executive secretary of the NAACP and had clashed repeatedly with other leaders and organizations. He was not a supporter of the kind of direct-action protest that other organizations engaged in. Lewis's experience of Wilkins was that he had a holier-than-thou attitude and thought himself above everyone else, except Randolph. He was also jealous of King and felt that the NAACP was not getting the attention and funding it deserved as a long-running civil rights organization. According to Lewis:

> [Wilkins] seemed to assume that because he was the head of the largest organization among us in terms of sheer membership … he was the master and we were nothing but a bunch of upstarts. He clearly assumed that we were naïve … including Dr. King. He didn't trust us young people in SNCC … but he didn't trust Dr. King either. He seemed to feel that King was basically a careless, unsophisticated, country preacher, and to envy the power and position Dr. King had attained. He didn't think he deserved it.[3]

Wilkins was closely allied with Whitney Young, leader of the National Urban League. Young's organization focused on employment opportunities for black Americans as well as federal aid for cities. Young was more of an administrator and fundraiser than a grassroots activist, and while Lewis respected the work of Young's organization, he did not view him as a movement-oriented leader. Along with Wilkins, Young's approach to the march was as a show of solidarity with the Kennedy administration's proposed civil rights legislation.

James Farmer was the director of CORE and had worked closely with Lewis and SNCC during the Freedom Rides of 1961. Farmer and Lewis had had their disagreements in the past—most notably when Farmer opted to withdraw participation in the rides after violence in Alabama—but among the Big Six group they (and their organizations) shared a very similar ideology and a more hands-on approach to activism than the other, more conservative, leaders.

John Lewis was the youngest member of the group. Many in his organization did not support the march and did not think SNCC should take part in it. They believed it "would be a lame event, organized by the cautious, conservative traditional power structure of black America, in compliance with and most likely under the control of the federal government" and that it would not represent the kind of direct action SNCC stood for: using nonviolent methods to disrupt the status quo and call national attention to the plight of black Americans.[4] SNCC members believed that if they were to take part in the event, it should be on their own terms, which included protests, sit-ins, and mass arrests around Washington.

Lewis himself thought the march was a good idea. While some members of SNCC believed participation in the march was equal to an endorsement of President Kennedy, Lewis did not view it as a declaration of support for the administration generally or the civil rights bill specifically. Instead, he saw it as an "opportunity to highlight what we were doing and facing with our direct action all throughout the South, a chance yet again to call the nation's attention to the ugliness and violence and suffering."[5]

Despite the differing approaches of the other Big Six leaders, Lewis was determined that SNCC should be represented so that they could have a voice. Unlike the other Big Six members, Lewis and Farmer saw the march as a means of nonviolent protest against the Kennedy administration, which had to this point been all talk and no real action when it came to civil rights legislation. This criticism of the administration would be a sticking point between Lewis and the more conservative members of the group.

The March on Washington for Jobs and Freedom took place on August 28, 1963, in Washington, DC. Over 250,000 people participated in what was then the largest civil rights demonstration in US history. The event began with a rally at the Washington Monument. It featured several musicians, including Bob Dylan, Joan Baez, and Mahalia Jackson. Demonstrators made the mile-long (1.6 km) march to the Lincoln Memorial, where members of the Big Six, along with other civil rights and religious leaders, gave speeches. Randolph gave the opening remarks, Lewis spoke fourth, and the last speech of the day was Dr. King's famous "I Have a Dream" speech. At the end of the day, the Big Six and others met with President Kennedy at the White House.

Growing Apart

As membership in SNCC grew and new members vastly outnumbered the original core Nashville group, Lewis's relationship with his organization began to deteriorate. Many were displeased by the concessions he made at the March on Washington, but the real turning point for Lewis and SNCC started in 1964, after the Mississippi Freedom Summer voter registration campaign.

During this campaign, membership in the organization swelled to include many white liberal students from the North. There were several people within SNCC who were beginning to disapprove of white participation, especially in any sort of leadership role. SNCC had always been an interracial

JOHN LEWIS'S
ORIGINAL SPEECH

The speech John Lewis gave at the March on Washington was not the one he wanted to give. The original version was much more explicitly critical of the Kennedy administration's inaction on civil rights as well as more aggressive in tone when it came to direct action. While Lewis was and always has been a proponent of nonviolence, some of his words were seen as far too militant for some members of the Big Six as well as other participants in the march.

A copy of Lewis's speech was circulated the evening before the march and reached Archbishop Patrick O'Boyle, who was so offended that he called the White House and threatened to pull out of the march. The archbishop's main issue was the line "patience is a dirty and nasty word," because it went against the Catholic belief that patience is a virtue, so Lewis agreed to remove it. However, the next day, as the march was already in progress, Lewis was forced to rewrite other portions of his speech in a security guard's office behind the Lincoln Memorial statue. March leaders were gathered there, and Wilkins was especially angry. King did not have a problem with it, and other SNCC members in attendance told Lewis not to change a single word, but ultimately he decided to make the changes at the request of Randolph, for whom he had the utmost respect.

Cut portions of Lewis's original speech include: "which side is the federal government on?"; "We will not wait for the President, the Justice Department, nor Congress, but we will take matters into our own hands and create a source of power, outside of any national structure, that could and would assure us a victory"; and "We will march through the South, through the heart of Dixie, the way Sherman did. We shall pursue our own 'scorched earth' policy and burn Jim Crow to the ground—nonviolently."[6]

John Lewis speaks at the March on Washington for Jobs and Freedom.

Despite the concessions he was forced to make, Lewis felt the speech was a success, and his was certainly the most militant of the day. Still, he faced criticism from members of his organization and others who believed he had compromised his message by changing his original speech to appease others.

organization, and Lewis believed wholeheartedly that it should remain so, and that to segregate the organization was antithetical to their goals. However, many new members—most notably Stokely Carmichael, who would replace Lewis as chairman in 1966—were proponents of black nationalism and did not want white people involved in the organization.

Many new members also did not subscribe to the philosophy of nonviolence, instead believing that self-defense was a more appropriate response to the widespread violence faced by black Americans. The rift between these factions widened as the group grew larger and more geographically spread out. Initially, SNCC was a small, close-knit group; everyone knew each other and trusted each other. As it grew larger and people of differing experiences and viewpoints joined, the intimacy and trust that was so essential to SNCC's success was practically nonexistent.

The size of the organization was also a problem in terms of leadership. Unlike other organizations, SNCC was formed with decentralized leadership. No one person or small group of people could make decisions for the entire organization; everything was done by consensus. This leadership strategy was untenable given the increased and spread-out membership, and people within the organization began jockeying for power—something Lewis never did and was very uncomfortable with, feeling it was against SNCC's founding principles.

The Freedom Summer took a physical and mental toll on the volunteers, especially because they did not make any significant progress in terms of voting rights legislation. People were tired and fed up with the government's inaction on these issues. Many within the organization started to turn away from the government completely, no longer believing that trying to work within the system would accomplish anything. Lewis understood their position but did not share it. He

Stokely Carmichael, who replaced Lewis as chairman of SNCC in 1966, was a proponent of black nationalism and clashed with Lewis over the direction SNCC should take.

would continue to work with both the federal government and more conservative civil rights organizations. Ultimately, he would perhaps effect the most change from within the federal government as a congressman.

CHAPTER FOUR

Getting in the Way

J ohn Lewis has spent his life fighting for equality, but he is best known for his actions during the 1960s civil rights struggle. Lewis was a participant in the Freedom Rides, the Mississippi Freedom Summer, and the Selma march—events that directly led to the passage of the nation's most important civil rights legislation. Lewis's mother taught him from a young age that, for his own personal safety, he should not get in white people's way. However, his oft-repeated goal of "finding a way to get in the way" was firmly established during this period, which saw real change in the face of tremendous adversity and violence.

Lewis poses next to his arrest records and various mugshots after being awarded the Nashville Public Library Literary Award in 2016.

The Boynton Decision

The 1960 case *Boynton v. Virginia* is a lesser-known but significant legal battle of the civil rights movement. In it, the US Supreme Court ruled that all segregation in interstate travel—including facilities (i.e., restrooms, waiting areas, and ticket counters)—was unconstitutional. This ruling was an extension of the 1946 case *Morgan v. Virginia*, in which the Supreme Court ruled that segregation on interstate buses violated the Constitution's commerce clause, which gives power over interstate travel laws to the federal government and not to individual states.

Lewis wrote to SCLC cofounder Fred Shuttlesworth in Birmingham, Alabama, with the idea to test the facilities at the Greyhound station there and see if the *Boynton* desegregation ruling was being implemented. Shuttlesworth wrote back telling Lewis that it was not a good idea since the racial climate in Birmingham was already too volatile. Luckily, CORE was already planning a *Boynton* test case and placed an ad in the SNCC newspaper, the *Student Voice*, looking for volunteers for what they were calling Freedom Ride 1961. Lewis applied immediately, and in his application he wrote that "human dignity is the most important thing in my life. This is the most important decision in my life, to decide to give up all if necessary for the Freedom Ride, that Justice and Freedom might come to the Deep South."[1] Lewis was selected as one of thirteen riders—seven black and six white—to make the journey from Washington, DC, to New Orleans, Louisiana.

Freedom Riders

CORE founder James Farmer organized the 1961 Freedom Ride. Farmer was one of the seven black riders and would later join Lewis as one of the Big Six. On May 4, 1961, Lewis, Farmer, and the rest of the riders headed to the DC bus terminal, where they split into two interracial, mixed-gender groups. Six riders, including Lewis, boarded a Greyhound bus, and the other seven took a Trailways bus. The itinerary for both trips was to make stops at terminals in Virginia, North Carolina, South Carolina, Georgia, Alabama, Mississippi, and to end the trip in New Orleans, Louisiana, on May 17—the anniversary of the *Brown* decision.

The group did not face any significant trouble in Virginia or North Carolina but encountered their first real opposition in Rock Hill, South Carolina, on May 9. Rock Hill had been the location of several sit-ins and mass protestor arrests the previous year, and racial tensions were high. The Rock Hill terminal still had not desegregated their facilities, and when Lewis attempted to use the whites-only bathroom, he was verbally threatened by a group of young white men waiting at the station. When he refused to use the "colored" bathroom, the men physically assaulted him. One of the white riders, Al Bigelow, put himself in between Lewis and his attackers and was beaten as well. Genevieve Hughes, a white female rider, stepped in and was thrown to the ground by one of the attackers. At this point, a police officer (who had been standing by doing nothing throughout the attack) stepped in and told the group of white men to leave, but made no arrests. The group on the Trailways bus, which was several hours behind the Greyhound, arrived at Rock Hill later that day and found that the terminal was closed and locked.

After the attack, Lewis was taken to Friendship Junior College and found a telegram waiting for him. He learned that his application for a foreign-service position had been accepted, and he was scheduled for a finalist interview the following day in Philadelphia. He had applied to the program run by the American Friends Service Committee (the Quakers) because he wanted to travel to Africa and reconnect with his heritage. It was a difficult decision, but he decided to go to Philadelphia for the interview. He was accepted, not to the Africa position but to one in India, which would begin in late summer 1961. He accepted it and traveled back down South to meet back up with the riders, in Birmingham.

Before he could rejoin the group, he learned that the Greyhound bus, which had taken on several new volunteers in

A group of Freedom Riders sits outside a burned-out Greyhound bus, which was attacked by a white mob in Anniston, Alabama. This was just one of many violent incidents faced during their 1961 campaign to desegregate bus terminal facilities.

Atlanta, had been attacked by a mob, including several KKK members, in Anniston, Alabama. The mob had learned of their arrival and was waiting at the station, where they slashed the bus's tires. The bus driver locked the door and left the station, followed by the mob, but was forced to stop a few miles outside of town when the tires went flat. The mob attacked the bus, breaking the windows and throwing a firebomb inside. The passengers were able to escape before the bus blew up but were attacked once outside. Finally, Alabama state troopers arrived and got the mob to disperse, but no arrests were made. The Greyhound riders were all too injured to continue, but most of them were denied care at the local hospital.

Meanwhile, the Trailways bus had had some Klansmen on board since its departure from Anniston. The Klansmen taunted and beat the riders on the journey to Birmingham. When the bus arrived at the Trailways station in Birmingham, they were met by a white mob even bigger than the one that met the Greyhound bus in Anniston. The Birmingham mob beat the Trailways riders with baseball bats, lead pipes, and bicycle chains. There were many reporters on the scene, and they were also attacked. One of the most viciously beaten riders that day was Jim Peck, a white man, who had his face kicked in and his teeth knocked out during the assault.

Birmingham's police chief Eugene "Bull" Connor was closely aligned with the KKK and allowed the violence to go on unchecked for fifteen minutes. No police presence was anywhere near the station until the allotted time had passed. The Birmingham police were aware of this planned attack, but they did nothing to stop it. Later, Connor would claim that the lack of police intervention was because it was Mother's Day and the officers were given time off to be with their families.

Not Backing Down

The Alabama attacks were covered in the national news with the now iconic photographs of the burning bus and bloodied riders, but the media attention was not enough to ensure safety going forward. At this point, James Farmer decided to call off the rest of the trip. Most of the riders were too injured to continue, and they would only face certain violence the deeper south they went. Lewis, who had rejoined the riders, wholeheartedly disagreed with Farmer's decision, which went against everything he believed in:

> [Farmer's decision] defied one of the most basic tenets of nonviolent action ... that there can be no surrender in the face of brute force or any form of violent opposition ... To back down would effectively end the entire civil rights movement ... It would tell those in the South and anywhere else in the nation who respond with their fists and weapons to opposition that violence *can* put an end to peaceful protest.[2]

Diane Nash and other members of the Nashville movement agreed with Lewis and decided to continue the journey with ten new volunteers from SNCC.

Marching On

The national attention the Alabama attacks received put pressure on the Kennedy administration to address the situation. In response, President Kennedy ordered the Alabama authorities to protect the riders. However, Birmingham police, led by Connor, detained the Freedom Riders at the Birmingham bus station and then arrested them for what Connor claimed was their own protection. They were jailed for two days before being released in the middle of the night, driven to the Alabama/Tennessee border, and left on the side of the road deep in Klan territory. Luckily, the group was able to find a local black couple to take them in for the night as they made preparations to return to Birmingham the following day.

By May 19, more volunteers arrived in Birmingham, and there were now twenty-one Freedom Riders prepared to leave on a 3:00 p.m. bus to Montgomery. However that bus, and those that followed, were all canceled because there were no drivers willing to take them. There was a large mob at the Birmingham terminal, but the police were present, and no physical violence occurred. Meanwhile, US Attorney General Robert F. Kennedy was negotiating with both Alabama authorities and the Greyhound terminal manager to try to get a driver and safe passage for the riders to Montgomery.

The morning of May 20, a bus carrying only the Freedom Riders left Birmingham for Montgomery with a Birmingham police escort. When they reached the city limits, the Alabama highway patrol took over the escort until the bus reached Montgomery's city limits, at which point it was abandoned by all police protection.

When they pulled into the Montgomery terminal, there was a group of reporters and a small group of white men present. However, once the riders exited the bus, they were quickly swarmed by a mob of people—white men, women, and even children—brandishing weapons. The media was attacked first and then the riders, especially white rider Jim Zwerg. Lewis was beaten and knocked unconscious. The mob even attacked John Siegenthaler, an aide sent to Alabama by the Kennedys to help ensure the riders' safety. President Kennedy, who had been monitoring the situation closely since the violence made national news, sent hundreds of federal marshals to Montgomery to restore order.

On the evening of May 21, there was a mass gathering at Montgomery's First Baptist Church. Dr. Martin Luther King Jr. was set to address the crowd. Outside, a white mob rioted, throwing rocks and firebombs into the church. Federal marshals held them back, preventing further vicious attacks. Finally, Alabama governor John Malcolm Patterson declared martial law and sent in the Alabama National Guard, who dispersed the mob but then held everyone inside the church, claiming it was for their own safety.

Freedom Riders John Lewis (*left*) and Jim Zwerg (*right*) are pictured after being viciously attacked at a Montgomery, Alabama, bus station on May 20, 1961

Despite the threat of more violence, the riders continued on to Jackson, Mississippi. They were given protection on the way, but once they arrived in Jackson, they were promptly arrested. After two weeks in county jails, they were transported to Parchman Farm—the most notorious prison farm in Mississippi. The Freedom Riders were not physically harmed by order of the Mississippi governor, who did not want the bad publicity, but the guards did everything in their power to make them as uncomfortable as possible to try to break their spirits. For example, they were given only minimal clothing to wear—just a T-shirt and shorts with no socks, shoes, or long pants. They were not allowed any time outside their cells, were denied reading material (except the Bible), and were only allowed to shower twice a week. They were sprayed with water from a fire hose in their cells and then blasted with fans to make them freezing cold. On especially hot days, the windows were left closed. Prison officials also left the lights on day and night to make sleep difficult.

Getting Out the Vote

While at Parchman, Lewis decided that not only was he going to cancel his trip to India, but he no longer wanted to be a minister and would not finish his studies at American Baptist. After being released from Parchman on July 7, 1961, Lewis decided to commit to civil rights activism full-time. The experience of the Freedom Rides had called national attention to the movement and showed Lewis how far they still had to go. He was fully committed to working toward that goal within the movement. Lewis returned to Nashville and continued the work of desegregating the city, focusing on businesses such as movie theaters and hotels that had segregated facilities. He also enrolled at Fisk University to study philosophy and get a deeper knowledge of the type of things he learned in James Lawson's workshops.

Soon after Lewis returned to Nashville, SNCC held a leadership workshop to discuss the direction of future activism. President Kennedy had met with SNCC and CORE members in June and pledged funding if they would focus their efforts on registering black voters as opposed to continuing their highly visible protests and demonstrations. SNCC was divided on the issue and did not initially shift their focus, but within a few years they would lead the charge for voter registration in the Deep South.

More than any other state in the South, Mississippi was the worst in terms of race relations and voter suppression. The state had a large black population, especially in rural farming areas, but before the 1964 Freedom Summer campaign only around 5 percent of eligible black voters were registered. SNCC member Bob Moses had been working as a field secretary in Mississippi since 1961 trying to register black voters. He was one of very few people working in Mississippi at that time and faced significant resistance from local authorities and white supremacists in the area.

The Council of Federated Organizations (COFO), a coalition of the four major civil rights groups—SNCC, CORE, SCLC, and the NAACP—organized the Freedom Summer campaign. SNCC was the most active of the four, followed by CORE, but there was very minimal participation from the SCLC and NAACP. The goal of the Freedom Summer campaign was to encourage and assist black Mississippians to register to vote in a place where they faced intense voter suppression.

There were several components to the Freedom Summer project. The first was voter registration. SNCC volunteers went door-to-door, into the fields, and to community hubs such as churches and black businesses all around the state. They talked to locals about the importance of voting and what their rights were as United States citizens. By embedding themselves in these communities and fostering relationships with the people, SNCC volunteers hoped to both educate and help black Mississippians overcome their very legitimate fear of the dangers facing them if they tried to exercise their voting rights. Violent reprisal was just one of these dangers; it was a common practice for the names of applicants to be published in local newspapers, leading to economic sanctions such as loss of employment and housing, as well as banks calling in loans for black business owners. This extended not just to those trying to register themselves, but to their family members as well. White authorities also punished the entire black community for the actions of a few by shutting down the commodities program, a part of President Lyndon Johnson's War on Poverty initiative, in which the government provided food to impoverished rural areas.

The second part was the freedom schools, which provided educational opportunities not available to Mississippi's black population. SNCC volunteers taught not only civics and citizenship rights but also reading, writing, typing, math, and black history and literature. They also operated freedom clinics that provided health care to communities with little to no access to doctors, as well as to people who could not afford treatment even if they did have a health-care facility nearby.

It was clear that an organized, large-scale campaign was needed to call attention to voter suppression in Mississippi. It

Three Democratic congressmen meet with a group of SNCC workers in Greenwood, Mississippi, during the 1964 Freedom Summer voter registration campaign.

was also clear that they would need a large number of volunteers. Some people in SNCC, including Bob Moses and John Lewis, believed it was important to recruit and train white college students from the North, both because they needed extra people and because young white participants would bring much-needed attention to the project. This idea was unpopular with other SNCC members who believed that white participation was problematic in several ways. White participants tended to get the credit for the work done by the black majority, and even well-intentioned white volunteers tended to take leadership roles they had not earned. Most troubling to some was the image that white participation would project to those outside the movement.

SNCC was founded on the principle of nurturing independence and self-reliance among the black Southerners. White involvement raised "the question of perpetuating the image of racial dependence, that somehow black people need whites to get anything done" and some SNCC members felt that having "white kids coming in to teach skills to impoverished blacks seemed to contradict that principle."[3] Ultimately, it was decided that white volunteers were necessary, and Lewis and others went recruiting at Northern colleges and universities. Volunteer orientation and training were held in Oxford, Ohio. The Northern students, who were predominately white, had no conception of how bad things were in the Deep South, and it was important to Lewis and SNCC that potential recruits be properly trained and aware of how dangerous the mission would be. All volunteers were fully informed of the dangers they might face, including physical harm, arrest, and possibly death. Their applications were thoroughly reviewed by SNCC members to make sure that they were up to the task. It was also made clear to the white students that their safety and the success of the mission would depend on them following the instructions of black leaders. Without mutual trust and respect, the project had no chance of success.

SNCC established headquarters in Greenwood and Jackson, Mississippi, as bases for operations, but the majority of volunteers would be out in rural areas, staying among the people, at prearranged safe houses. Given the danger involved, there were armed guards stationed outside many of these locations. Lewis disagreed with this but accepted it as a necessary evil because of the very real threat posed by Mississippi white supremacists. The increased civil rights activism in the state saw a surge in Klan membership and activity ahead of the Freedom Summer, and violence was all but assured over the course of the coming months.

The Freedom Summer Murders

At the beginning of the summer, before most people even made it down to Mississippi, everyone got a grim reminder of just how dangerous their mission was. Three volunteers—Mickey Schwerner, Andy Goodman, and James Chaney—disappeared on a trip to Meridian, Mississippi, to investigate the burning of a local church where one of the freedom schools was located. Schwerner and Goodman, both white New Yorkers, and Chaney, a black Mississippi native, were stopped for speeding by the police in the nearby town of Philadelphia, taken to jail, and never heard from again. The car they were driving was found burned out, but there was no sign of the three men.

Immediately after hearing the news, Lewis traveled to Mississippi with a group of other leaders and demanded information from the local authorities. The authorities were uncooperative and did not allow them to visit the burned church or see the recovered car.

The disappearance was widely publicized, leading President Johnson to instruct the FBI, US Navy, and local authorities to investigate the disappearance. The bodies were not recovered until early August as a result of an anonymous tip, and the investigation uncovered the participation of the local Klan, county sheriff's office, and local police. One month before the bodies were recovered, Johnson signed the Civil Rights Act of 1964 into law, on July 2.

The violence did not end with the deaths of Schwerner, Goodman, and Chaney. Over the course of the summer, there were hundreds of incidents including mass arrests, physical assaults, church burnings, and bombings. The murders brought national attention to what the activists were doing down in Mississippi and to the brave volunteers who worked through the Freedom Summer knowing that their lives were at stake.

Lewis worked tirelessly in many different roles. Ahead of the summer, he traveled around the country recruiting volunteers and training them once accepted. He was one of the lead organizers of the project, which required a great deal of coordination between volunteers as well as a network of safe houses and transportation. In Mississippi, he canvassed door-to-door in rural communities, encouraging the locals to attend one of their freedom schools and travel to the courthouse to register. As one of the most well-known activists, Lewis gave speeches around the state at voter registration rallies. He and the other volunteers would travel by night, often speeding and driving without headlights to get to their destinations because it was unsafe for white and black passengers to travel together during the day.

While not an immediate success, the Freedom Summer brought national attention to black voter disenfranchisement and violence in the South. By the end of the summer, more than seventeen thousand people had filled out voter registration forms, although only a small percentage were actually allowed to register.

Mississippi Freedom Democratic Party

The most ambitious component of the Freedom Summer campaign was the establishment of the Mississippi Freedom Democratic Party (MFDP), a parallel political party of majority black delegates organized to challenge the validity of the all-white delegation of Mississippi Democrats. Registered black Democrats had been barred from participating in county and state meetings to elect the delegates in violation of the national Democratic Party rules for delegate selection. In response, the black voters held their own elections (in accordance with the party rules) that were open to registered Democrats regardless of race. The resulting sixty-eight MFDP delegates—four white and sixty-four black—planned to attend the Democratic National Convention in Atlantic City, New Jersey, in August 1964. Part of Lewis's work during the Freedom Summer was traveling around the state to rally support for the MFDP.

The MFDP was not ultimately successful in getting any delegate seats, but their presence at the convention, especially a televised speech by delegate Fannie Lou Hamer, brought even more attention to the cause. Hamer's speech was cut off by President Johnson, who feared losing the Southern vote if the MFDP delegates were seated. He tried to negotiate a compromise with the MFDP in which they would receive two seats (and he would choose the delegates seated). Dr. King, Bayard Rustin, and Roy Wilkins urged the MFDP to accept this offer, but Lewis and SNCC did not. The MFDP unanimously voted to reject Johnson's offer and staged a sit-in on the convention floor.

Bloody Sunday

After the stress of the Freedom Summer, SNCC was in disarray, with many people feeling disillusioned and frustrated at the government's inaction. Although a significant piece of legislation, the Civil Rights Act of 1964 had made no provisions for voting rights. Lewis looked to Selma, Alabama, as a way to bring everyone together for a common purpose. SNCC had

FANNIE LOU HAMER

Fannie Lou Hamer was one of the most outspoken and committed of all the Mississippi residents attempting to register. SNCC visited her in 1962, and when she tried to register and organize others in her community to do the same, she was denied and lost her job. She was the target of a drive-by shooting and forced to leave her home for safety. In 1963, she became a SNCC field secretary and was active in the group's efforts to educate and register black voters in her home state. Hamer became the vice chair of the delegation of the Mississippi Freedom Democratic Party and gave a rousing speech at the 1964 Democratic convention, where she posited: "if the Freedom Democratic Party is not seated now, I question America. Is this America, the land of the free and the home of the brave, where we have to sleep with our telephones off the hooks because our lives be threatened daily, because we want to live as decent human beings, in America?"[4] The MFDP was not successful that year, but Hamer continued to work tirelessly for voting rights and political representation for African Americans. Members of the MFDP were successfully seated as delegates at the 1968 convention, and Hamer was elected as a national party delegate in 1972.

already been working in Selma since 1963, trying to register black voters, and had been effectively shut down by the local authorities in 1964 when they issued an injunction banning the gathering of more than three civil rights activists. This did not deter activists, though. The SCLC officially took over the Selma voter registration campaign in January 1965. Many in SNCC were angry that King and the SCLC had come in after SNCC had laid all the groundwork in previous years. As he was also a member of the SCLC, Lewis understood their frustrations but respected what King and the SCLC were trying to do.

In addition to the injunction against civil rights activists, Selma Sheriff Jim Clark had deputized and armed Selma's white citizens. A coalition of SCLC members, a small group of SNCC members, and the local Dallas County Voters League organized demonstrations to begin in late January 1965 at the county courthouse where the registrar was located.

At that time in Selma, only 2 percent of African Americans were registered to vote. Potential voters could only attempt to register on the first and third Mondays of each month, where they would have to stand in line and get a copy of the literacy test, which was designed for them to fail. Even on the days the registrar was open, there was no guarantee anyone would even be allowed to take the test, much less successfully register.

Lewis and King led a series of demonstrations, beginning January 18, when hundreds of people marched from Brown's Chapel Church to the courthouse steps. There they were met with armed resistance from local authorities and local militia. They were forced to line up in an alley next to the courthouse, and no one was allowed inside. On the second day, violence and mass arrests began. The campaign continued on this way for weeks and reached its boiling point at the end of February, when civil rights activist Jimmie Lee Jackson was shot and

John Lewis (*right*) and Hosea Williams (*left*) lead a line of marchers in Selma, Alabama, on March 7, 1965. This day became known as "Bloody Sunday" after local authorities attacked the marchers on the Edmund Pettus Bridge.

killed by an Alabama state trooper while trying to protect his mother from a beating during a peaceful nighttime protest march. Jackson's death prompted the SCLC's James Bevel—Lewis's friend and former member of the Nashville group and SNCC—to suggest a march from Selma to Montgomery. Alabama governor George Wallace and local authorities were determined to stop this march at all costs.

SNCC members, especially executive secretary James Forman, did not support the idea of the march and decided not to participate in any significant way. They felt it would do more for King personally, further cementing him as the nation's most visible civil rights leader, than it would for the people of Selma. Lewis disagreed; he felt that the people of Selma needed the march as an outlet for their anger and pain, but in his position as chairman of SNCC he was obligated to sign the official letter stating that SNCC would not participate. However, he believed in the march and so decided that he would participate—not as SNCC chairman but as John Lewis.

On March 7, 1965, Lewis led the march alongside SCLC's Hosea Williams. Dr. King had opted not to participate in the march on this day because he had received what were considered credible death threats. Instead, he returned to Atlanta. Lewis and Williams led over six hundred marchers, two abreast, from the church. When they reached the highest point of the Edmund Pettus Bridge, they saw hundreds of people—including state troopers, sheriff's deputies, and civilians—gathered to block their path. Major John Cloud ordered them to turn around and return to their homes or their church and gave them two minutes to do so. Lewis and Williams knelt in prayer, and before they had a chance to retreat, the authorities moved in. Lewis was clubbed and his skull fractured by a state trooper; the marchers were teargassed, beaten, and trampled by mounted police. Reporters caught live footage of this scene, which would come to be known as "Bloody Sunday," and it aired nationally on ABC that evening.

Selma to Montgomery

The national outrage over the violent scene in Selma prompted President Johnson to take concrete action. On March 15, he delivered a speech to a joint session of Congress, calling for legislation to protect the voting rights of African Americans. Johnson stated:

> What happened in Selma is part of a far larger movement which reaches into every section and state of America. It is the effort of American Negroes to accrue for themselves the full blessings of American life. Their cause must be our cause too. Because it's not just Negroes, but really it's all of us who must overcome the crippling legacy of bigotry and injustice. And we shall overcome.[5]

Organizers were determined that a march would take place. The injunction against the march was lifted, and on March 21, under the protection of the Alabama National Guard, the US Army, and federal marshals, over three thousand people set out from Selma for the five-day march to Montgomery. Marchers walked for most of the day and camped out in fields overnight. When they finally reached the state capitol building, John Lewis was right out in front.

Five months later, on August 6, 1965, President Lyndon Johnson signed the Voting Rights Act of 1965. Section 2 of the act explicitly states that "no voting qualification or prerequisite to voting, or standard, practice, or procedure shall be imposed or applied by any State or political subdivision to deny or abridge the right of any citizen of the United States to vote on account of race or color."[6] This legislation had an immediate effect, with the number of registered African Americans in the United States increasing from approximately 23 percent before the act to 61 percent by 1969. The ability to exercise their voting rights directly led to the election of African Americans to government offices on the local, state, and national levels. Soon, John Lewis would be among them.

CHAPTER FIVE

From Activist to Politician

The work of John Lewis and his contemporaries was directly responsible for the major civil rights legislation of the 1960s. Long before Lewis was a politician himself, he had relationships with high-level political figures. He did not always agree with the men in power, but through his work and his personal relationships with them—especially Bobby Kennedy—he was able to change them on a personal level. He was also able to change the everyday lives of black Americans in the South and, soon, he would come to represent the interests of the people of Georgia's Fifth District in Atlanta.

Lewis (*far left*) is pictured with his mentor and friend Dr. Martin Luther King Jr. (*far right*) during the March on Washington for Jobs and Freedom.

Acts for Change

Lewis was only twenty-six years old when he left SNCC and had an entire life of work ahead of him, but he—along with the countless other courageous men and women who stood strong in the face of racial hatred—was already directly responsible for two of the most significant pieces of legislation in United States history. After the assassination of President Kennedy in 1963, his successor, Lyndon B. Johnson, quickly passed the civil rights legislation that Kennedy had championed before his untimely death. The Civil Rights Act of 1964 stated, "All persons shall be entitled to the full and equal enjoyment of the goods, services, facilities, and privileges, advantages, and accommodations of any place of public accommodation, as defined in this section, without discrimination or segregation on the ground of race, color, religion, or national origin."[1] Restaurants, theaters, hotels, parks, and many other formerly segregated facilities were now open to everyone. The act also banned discrimination in employment based on race, gender, religion, or national origin, and created an Equal Employment Opportunity Commission to oversee any such employment disputes. The 1964 act also addressed voting inequalities but, as was made abundantly clear in Mississippi and Alabama, a stronger and more comprehensive piece of legislation was needed to ensure equal voting rights for all Americans.

In the wake of the violence in Selma, Johnson signed the Voting Rights Act of 1965. This legislative work banned literacy tests, offered federal oversight of voter registration in places where less than 50 percent of the nonwhite population had not registered to vote, and allowed the US attorney general to investigate the use of poll taxes in state and local elections. Poll taxes, fees that had to be paid before a person was eligible to vote, were already banned in federal elections in 1964, and in 1966, the Supreme Court banned them in state elections as well. Many civil rights leaders, including Lewis, were present at the signing ceremony of the act on August 6, 1965. Lewis and others had put their lives on the line (and many of those lives had been lost for the cause), and this law seemed like the culmination of all they had fought so hard for. While the law did have an immediate and lasting effect, it was not enough to fully counteract new voter suppression tactics that emerged in the following decades.

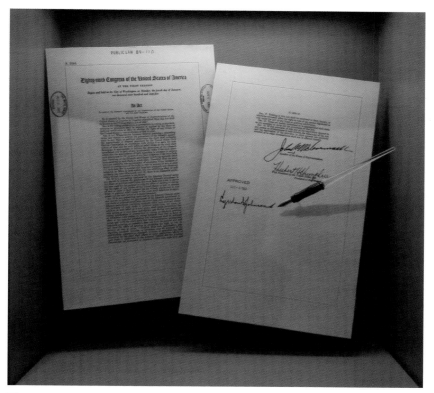

The Voting Rights Act of 1965, and the pen with which President Lyndon B. Johnson signed it into law, is displayed at the International Civil Rights Center & Museum in Greensboro, North Carolina.

On the Campaign Trail

By the late 1960s, Lewis had emerged as someone much different than he had been at the start of the decade. Initially uninterested about the presidential election of 1960, he had changed his tune and directed his attention and his support to politics by the 1970s.

When Kennedy was running for office in 1960, Lewis had focused on grassroots work and felt that mainstream politics was "distant and irrelevant compared to the direct action we were involved in ... Nothing about [John F. Kennedy or Richard Nixon] connected directly to what we and other students were doing throughout the South."[2] Over the course of the next few years, his opinion on politics—and certain politicians—changed dramatically. He came to believe in the power of the vote and the importance of political participation. He had seen firsthand that the hearts and minds of politicians could be swayed if they were forced to really look at the problems facing the nation's most vulnerable citizens.

In the latter half of the 1960s, the country's attention was turned to the escalating war in Vietnam. As a conscientious objector, Lewis was against the war, but not only because of his nonviolent philosophy. He saw that black soldiers were disproportionately being sent to the front lines and that the massive amount of resources being used in the war were taking away from Johnson's domestic programs to combat ongoing economic and social inequality. Lewis's views on the war were shared by many, including Bobby Kennedy, who had been elected as US Senator from New York in 1964.

Lewis and Kennedy had a long history stretching back to the Freedom Rides. Initially, Lewis did not believe that either Bobby or his brother John Kennedy were truly committed to

Bobby Kennedy credited John Lewis and the student movement with opening his eyes to the reality of racial inequality in America.

the cause. In the early years of the movement, the Kennedys seemed to be more talk than action when it came to civil rights issues, concerned more with gaining the black vote than with the living experience of black Americans. However, over the years, Lewis saw a real change, especially in Bobby Kennedy, who had come to truly understand the civil rights struggle and believed in the necessity of substantive change. He specifically credited Lewis and the student movement with opening his eyes to the issues facing black Americans. Lewis recalls that, at a meeting in then-Attorney General Bobby Kennedy's office before the March on Washington, Kennedy said to him, "John, I now understand. The young people, the students have educated me."[3] From that point on, Lewis believed Kennedy was truly invested in the cause.

When Bobby Kennedy decided to run for president in the 1968 election, Lewis believed in his vision for change. Kennedy campaigned on a platform of racial and economic equality with a focus on eliminating poverty and crime, as well as opposition to Johnson's aggressive Vietnam War policy. Lewis was against Vietnam as well and had cofounded the Southern Coordinating Committee to End the War in Vietnam in 1966. Kennedy visited impoverished areas around the nation and met with the people face-to-face. He was especially disturbed by his visit to the Mississippi Delta, where he encountered starving children.

Lewis decided to join Kennedy's campaign and help mobilize black voters during the primary. It was during Kennedy's primary campaign, while readying for a rally in Indianapolis, Indiana, on April 4, 1968, that Lewis learned that Dr. King had been killed. That evening, Kennedy gave a heartfelt speech to the crowd, informing them of King's death. It moved Lewis, who was devastated by the murder of his friend and mentor. But Lewis still had hope in Bobby Kennedy. On King's death,

Lewis wrote that it was "all the more important for me to put everything I had into Kennedy's campaign. I saw this as the final extension of the movement. I transferred all the loyalty I had left from Dr. King to Bobby Kennedy."[4] Sadly, this hope was short-lived.

Lewis campaigned hard for Kennedy in California. He teamed up with labor organizer and activist Cesar Chavez, going door-to-door in the black and Hispanic neighborhoods of Los Angeles and talking to the people individually and at rallies. Their efforts paid off, and Kennedy won the California primary, largely due to the black and Hispanic vote. Late that evening, on June 5, 1968, just after giving his victory speech at

Lewis, accompanied by wife Lillian and son John-Miles, casts a vote for himself in the runoff election on September 2, 1986, at his polling place in Atlanta, Georgia.

the Hotel Ambassador, Bobby Kennedy was shot. He died of his injuries the next morning.

The loss of both King and Kennedy within a few weeks of each other had a devastating effect on Lewis and on the nation at large. It was a very dark time for Lewis on a personal level, but there was one bright spot: he married Lillian Miles a few days before Christmas 1968. In a few short years, they adopted a son, John-Miles Lewis.

Community Building

In the years between leaving SNCC and becoming a congressman, Lewis's main focus was on strengthening black communities across the nation. While the civil rights legislation solved some of the problems they faced, there was still widespread poverty as well as employment and housing inequality. The racism that existed before the civil rights movement did not just disappear after laws were passed; those who had been determined to keep black Americans as second-class citizens were still committed to doing so.

After leaving SNCC in 1966, Lewis briefly went north and worked as associate director of the Field Foundation, a civil rights and child welfare organization based in New York City. He was there a little over a year and returned south to Atlanta in 1967. That fall, he graduated from Fisk University and took a job as the director of the Community Organization Project (COP) with the Southern Regional Council. This interracial organization was dedicated to social justice and the elimination of racial discrimination. Lewis's work with COP focused on food, shelter, and employment in impoverished communities in rural and urban areas of the Deep South. "It was about showing people how to pool what money they had to form a bank of

LEWIS VISITS AFRICA

After the stress of the Freedom Summer, Lewis went on a SNCC-sponsored trip to Africa beginning in September 1964. At this time, many African countries had successfully liberated themselves from European colonial rule. These liberation movements were largely driven by young people, and Lewis and the other SNCC travelers with him admired what they were doing and were emboldened by their victories. Lewis traveled to Guinea, Liberia, Ghana, Ethiopia, Kenya, Zambia, and Egypt. Throughout his travels he saw black people in charge as pilots, policemen, bankers—things that were unthinkable in the South at the time. Lewis was inspired by his trip and the sense of freedom, independence, and human dignity he saw among the African people.

The SNCC contingent was only in Africa for three weeks, but Lewis and another traveler, Don Harris, extended their trip for another month and a half to give themselves more time to travel to different locations and talk to (and learn from) the people they met. Lewis learned that the young people of Africa did not know much about the American civil rights movement because US propaganda depicted it as a nation of racial harmony. Lewis and Harris spent time both educating people about their movement and learning about the Africans' own freedom struggles. In October, they attended an event that was the culmination of their trip: a weeklong independence celebration in Lusaka, Zambia. Lewis and Harris were elated as they watched, with a crowd of over 175,000 people, the newly elected Zambian president, Dr. Kenneth Kaunda, lower the British flag and raise the Zambian flag. Lewis returned to America determined to see black Americans experience that sense of liberation.

their own, a credit union. Or how to band together to buy groceries, or feed, or seed, in bulk amounts at low prices—how to form cooperatives."[5]

In 1970, Lewis took a position as executive director of the Voter Education Project. The VEP began in the early 1960s as an organization providing financial support to civil rights groups—including SNCC and the SCLC—working to register black voters. Under Lewis's direction, the organization moved beyond just funding programs and into more grassroots activism, including voter registration drives and educational seminars. Lewis also expanded the organization's scope beyond the African American communities to other poor and marginalized groups. His belief in the Beloved Community was very much a driving force behind this expansion. Lewis worked for the VEP for six years, and in that time, the number of black voters in the Deep South increased by two million. Many of those votes went to Jimmy Carter, who Lewis supported in the 1976 presidential election.

Taking ACTION

Lewis's first attempt at running for political office was the 1977 election for Georgia's Fifth District Congressional seat. He lost, but at this point in his life, he was determined to become a congressman.

Following the loss, he took a position in the Carter administration at ACTION, a federal agency dedicated to volunteer service. During his nomination hearing, Lewis expressed his desire to use the position as a way to extend the work he'd been doing for years "to tap into the spirit of the civil rights movement, to direct the agency's programs at a grassroots level, bringing our services to the disadvantaged and disabled as well as to minorities, going out into neighborhoods and communities and building a better society, a Beloved Community, literally block by block."[6] Lewis also oversaw domestic service programs with Volunteers in Service to America (VISTA), an anti-poverty program, and ran two programs for elderly volunteers, the Retired Senior Volunteer Program (RSVP) and the Foster Grandparent Program (FGP).

During his years with ACTION, Lewis traveled to the poorest regions of the nation, forming cooperatives in rural areas and working on revitalizing and fighting gentrification in urban areas. ACTION opened medical clinics in remote areas and improved conditions in nursing homes, orphanages, and homes for disabled children. Lewis was already familiar with Southern poverty; he grew up in it and had worked among the poor communities in the Deep South for his entire life. However, his time with ACTION expanded his understanding of poverty in America to include Native Americans, Hispanic people, and Appalachian whites.

For all the good he was able to do, his time with ACTION left him somewhat disillusioned with the Carter administration and its lack of tangible action when it came to America's poor. Lewis had personally written to President Carter telling him about what he'd seen within the coal-mining region of West Virginia. Lewis visited the area on behalf of ACTION in fall of 1979 and saw the poverty of the mining families firsthand. He went into the coal mines and the homes of mining families, many of whom were so poor they could barely afford food and clothing for their children. Lewis was shaken by the experience and wrote to President Carter, encouraging him to visit some of the places where ACTION was doing work to see what they were up against. Carter did not respond to Lewis's letter, and it left him frustrated that the president was not living up to the campaign promises he had made regarding welfare reform and job creation for America's poor. These were the same frustrations that Lewis heard from the American people during his travels—that they felt ignored by the federal government.

In addition to the lack of action, Lewis was growing tired of the bureaucratic red tape and political posturing he felt was getting in the way of doing the real work. He decided that it was time for him to work from the inside, as an elected official, and he returned to Atlanta to truly begin his political career.

Councilman to Congressman

When Lewis and his wife Lillian first purchased a home in Atlanta after their marriage, he began to understand some of the problems facing his city. He saw the housing discrimination in which neighborhoods were kept racially segregated. Real-estate agents would only show to white buyers in majority-white areas. In addition, lenders engaged in a discriminatory practice known as redlining, in which banks would deny mortgages to black applicants and insurance agencies would refuse coverage.

Lewis was elected to the Atlanta city council in 1981. His major concerns were white flight and the resulting de facto segregation in Atlanta's schools. White flight occurs when white people move from urban areas to the suburbs, resulting in abandoned homes and businesses, a depleted economy, and a shrinking tax base. Lewis was also concerned with ethics violations on the council related to conflicts of interest between council members' business dealings and their political decisions. While on the council, he pushed for legislation requiring public disclosure of the council members' sources of income. This was not popular with some people and made him an outsider on the council, but Lewis felt—as he had so many times in his life—

that it was the right thing to do, though it was not the easy thing to do. During Lewis's four-year term on the council, he was incredibly popular with the people in his district and had good relationships with both civilians and local authorities. He was reelected in 1985 with the support of 85 percent of voters.

In 1986, Lewis decided to run for congress again in Georgia's Fifth District, facing off against his longtime friend and fellow activist Julian Bond. Bond was the more experienced politician and was favored to win, but Lewis ran an aggressive campaign. Day and night, he was out in the city, talking to the voters in his district and holding

Civil rights activist and politician Julian Bond appears on primary election night in 1986.

community meetings. He was also very critical of Bond throughout the campaign, which would ultimately end their friendship. Bond won the most votes in the primary election but did not reach the majority required. As a result, there was a runoff election between Bond and Lewis, who received the second-most votes in the primary. It was a very close race, but in the end, Lewis beat Bond. He went on to easily defeat his Republican opponent in the general election, winning the congressional seat that he holds to this day.

CHAPTER SIX

The Conscience of the Congress

John Lewis's long history of fighting for the dispossessed and his refusal to compromise his moral code has earned him the nickname "the conscience of the US Congress." Since he was sworn in as a member of the US Congress in 1987, he has held his position as the House Representative for Georgia's Fifth District. During his long career, Lewis has continued to be a champion of civil rights for marginalized groups and is unafraid to speak out against injustice wherever he sees it. He has been arrested for acts of civil disobedience several times while he's been in office—once in 1988, outside the South African embassy where he was protesting apartheid-era racial repression, and again in 2006, in front of the Sudan embassy where he was protesting the

President Barack Obama presents John Lewis with the Presidential Medal of Freedom on February 15, 2011.

genocide in Darfur. His most recent arrest was in 2013 at an immigration-reform rally.

In 2017, Lewis made headlines after deciding to boycott the inauguration of then president-elect Donald Trump amid the controversy surrounding possible Russian involvement in the 2016 presidential election. In response, Trump accused Lewis via Twitter of being "All talk, talk, talk - no action or results." Many people, both Democrats and Republicans, took to social media to point out the many ways in which this statement is historically inaccurate. Not only is Lewis a man of action, those actions had results that have fundamentally changed the lives of many Americans. Even in his late seventies, Lewis is still out among the people, participating in acts of civil disobedience and getting into what he calls "good trouble."

Anti-War Positions

In the 1960s and 1970s, Lewis was a vocal critic of the Vietnam War. His distaste for America's aggressive military foreign policy continued in the decades that followed. In 1991, he stood on the floor of the House to oppose the Gulf War resolution authorizing the use of military force in Iraq. He also opposed the Iraq war from the very beginning in 2003, through its many escalations, and called for withdrawal on many occasions. On the Iraq war, Lewis pointed out the contradiction between waging war for the sake of peacekeeping in his 2012 book *Across That Bridge*:

> Our stated intention in Iraq ... was to rescue the Iraqi people from tyranny. Yet, after the tyrant was deposed and killed, we replaced one form of violence—a human dictator who reigned through

fear—with another. The people of Iraq are still not free from fear today, despite the claims that they are better off now. Because we used the same tools as the violator, the truth of the situation is obscured, making the victims defending themselves begin to look strangely similar to the aggressors they are defending themselves against.[1]

Lewis strongly believes that America needs to move away from a wartime economy and invest resources into building a peacetime economy, and that the resources used in war would be much better applied to the many domestic issues—including vast economic inequality—that the nation faces in the twenty-first century.

Regression of Voting Rights

In recent years, certain provisions of the Voting Rights Act have been challenged and overturned. In addition, questionable practices such as gerrymandering—the changing of district boundaries resulting in a demographic shift and an electorate that favors one party—have been used to manipulate election results. In 2013, the US Supreme Court ruled 5–4 in *Shelby County v. Holder* that part 4(b) of the Voting Rights Act was unconstitutional. The case, brought by Shelby County, Alabama, questions two interrelated parts of the act: Section 4(b) and Section 5. Section 4(b) defines specific voting districts with a history of voter discrimination. Section 5 prohibits the districts defined in 4(b) from changing their election laws and procedures without authorization from the federal government. The *Shelby* decision did not strike down Section 5 but declared Section 4(b) unconstitutional, which effectively nullifies Section 5. The court's argument was that the formula applied in Section 4(b) is based on a decades-old formula that is no longer applicable to current conditions.

In the aftermath of the *Shelby* decision, many states began implementing strict ID laws, with Texas doing so within one day of the ruling. Other methods of voter suppression that have been enacted in places since *Shelby* include: address requirements; reduced number of polling places; purging of voter rolls for those deemed ineligible; and the elimination of early voting, online registration, same-day registration, and preregistration for those under eighteen. The laws disproportionately affect African American, Latino, and Native American communities, especially the poor and elderly.

For John Lewis, who was on the front lines of the fight for voter equality, the *Shelby* decision was a huge blow. Lewis called this decision "a dagger in the heart of the Voting Rights Act." He has spoken out against this decision because he "disagrees with the court that the history of discrimination is somehow irrelevant today. The record clearly demonstrates numerous attempts to impede voting rights still exist, and it does not matter that those attempts are not as 'pervasive, widespread or rampant' as they were in 1965. One instance of discrimination is too much in a democracy."[2]

An Ally to the LGBTQ Community

Lewis's commitment to civil rights for all Americans had made him a champion of civil rights for the LGBTQ community. In 1996, he fought hard against the Defense of Marriage Act (DOMA). This act defined marriage as a legal union between a man and a woman. It gave states the right to deny acknowledging the validity of same-sex marriages. He gave a

John Lewis is a longtime ally to the LGBTQ community. He regularly shows his support by marching in and speaking at the yearly Atlanta Pride Parade in Atlanta, Georgia. This is the parade in 2011.

passionate speech defending the rights of same-sex couples on the House floor on July 11, 1996, in which he equated the struggle of black Americans during the civil rights movement to the current struggle of same-sex couples trying to exercise their basic human rights. One such human right is for a person to legally marry the person they love, regardless of sexual orientation. The law was passed over Lewis's objections, but the struggle for marriage equality did not end there.

In a 2003 op-ed for the *Boston Globe,* Lewis continued to express his disapproval over the legal discrimination against the LGBTQ community

> We cannot keep turning our backs on gay and lesbian Americans. I have fought too hard and too long against discrimination based on race and color not to stand up against discrimination based on sexual orientation. I've heard the reasons for opposing civil marriage for same-sex couples. Cut through the distractions, and they stink of the same fear, hatred, and intolerance I have known in racism and in bigotry. Some say let's choose another route and give gay folks some legal rights but call it something other than marriage. We have been down that road before in this country. Separate is not equal. The rights to liberty and happiness belong to each of us and on the same terms, without regard to either skin color or sexual orientation.[3]

It took many years, but same-sex marriage was finally fully legalized by the US Supreme Court in *Obergefell v. Hodges* in 2015. However, the fight for full equality for members of the LGBTQ community is far from over. In 2015, Lewis was a cosponsor of the proposed Equality Act that would explicitly extend all federal civil rights protections under the Civil Rights Act to include sexual orientation and gender identity. The Equality Act did not pass in 2015, nor in 2017 when it was reintroduced, but Lewis and the other cosponsors continue to push for civil rights legislation for the LGBTQ community today.

The most egregious discrimination in recent years has been directed at transgender Americans. In July 2017, President

Trump announced plans to ban transgender individuals from serving in the United States military. Lewis, who firmly opposes any discrimination based on gender identity, found it especially unconscionable to restrict the rights of Americans willing to put their lives on the line to serve their country.

Immigration Policy Reform

Lewis firmly believes that no human being is "illegal"—a word that is frequently used to describe immigrants. In the twenty-first century, immigration has been at the forefront of American politics. Lewis has cosponsored a number of immigration reform bills in Congress relating to immigrant child welfare and protection, protection of refugees and asylum seekers, detention and deportation policies, and pathways to citizenship.

On October 8, 2013, Lewis participated in a rally for immigration reform. The Camino Americano: March for Immigration Reform took place at the National Mall in Washington, DC. Lewis's presence there continued his long history of nonviolent civil disobedience and showed his support for a path to citizenship for America's immigrant population, as well as supporting a halt of the deportation of noncriminal immigrants and the separation of families. Lewis was arrested, alongside several other Democrats, for staging a sit-in blocking a street in front of the US Capitol Building.

Lewis continues to fight for the rights of immigrants, especially in the face of the Trump administration's zero-tolerance policy, enacted in 2018, which resulted in mass detention of immigrants at the US-Mexico border and the separation of children from their parents. Lewis spoke at a June 2018 Families Belong Together rally in Atlanta, Georgia, one of many held across the nation protesting the child

JOHN LEWIS: AUTHOR

As of 2018, John Lewis has published several books: two autobiographies and three graphic novels. His first autobiography, *Walking With the Wind: A Memoir of the Movement,* is a vividly detailed exploration of his life and work from his childhood up until the book's publication in 1998. His second, *Across That Bridge: A Vision for Change and the Future of America,* is a shorter but equally powerful book in which Lewis shares the wisdom he has accrued over the course of his life and discusses the principles of nonviolence on which he bases all his actions.

Beginning in 2013, Lewis (along with co-author Andrew Aydin and illustrator Nate Powell) published a series of graphic novels. The *March* trilogy is an illustrated memoir of Lewis's life from his boyhood through the major events of the civil rights movement. The idea for the *March* trilogy came from a comic book, *Martin Luther King and the Montgomery Story,* published by the Fellowship of Reconciliation in 1957. This comic influenced Lewis as a young activist, and he wanted to create something similar to tell his story. A new series, *Run,* was published in 2019 and picked up where the *March* trilogy left off, telling the story of Lewis's life after Selma. Graphic novels are powerful ways to visualize and appreciate key events in history and are gaining more popularity in the twenty-first century.

John Lewis has written a trilogy of graphic novels that illustrate the activism of his youth. Above, he signs a copy of *March: Book One* at a gala on the 150th anniversary of the Emancipation Proclamation.

separation and detention policy at the border. He also joined others in Congress who marched and staged a sit-in in front of the US Customs and Border Protection headquarters in Washington, DC.

Disarming Hate

In recent years, mass shootings have become terrifyingly commonplace in America, especially in schools and places of worship. Lewis is a very vocal proponent of gun control and reform. In the wake of the June 12, 2016, mass shooting at an Orlando, Florida, nightclub, Lewis led a twenty-five-hour sit-in on the House floor, chanting "No bill, no break!" and calling for a vote on gun-control legislation that would extend background checks and ban gun sales to people on the government's no-fly list.

On February 14, 2018, a mass shooting took place at Marjory Stoneman Douglas High School in Parkland, Florida. The Parkland student survivors have been some of the most outspoken activists for gun control legislation. Within weeks, the students organized the March for Our Lives rally in Washington, DC, and satellite marches took place all across the country in solidarity. Lewis was not much older than the Parkland students when he began to take direct action for change, and he spoke at the satellite rally in Atlanta, praising and encouraging the younger generation of activists. Lewis spoke of losing John F. Kennedy, Dr. King, and Bobby Kennedy to gun violence and addressed the fact that he is proud that the National Rifle Association (NRA) gave him an F—a rating from the organization that designates a politician as "a true enemy of gun owners' rights." He spoke of his forty-five arrests and his willingness to go to jail again

Lewis marches at the March for Our Lives gun control rally in Atlanta on March 24, 2018. This was one of many rallies across the nation organized in response to the February 14, 2018, mass shooting at a high school in Parkland, Florida.

in the fight against gun violence. He stressed the importance of the youth vote and urged the students "to march, to speak out, to find a way to get in the way ... You must never give up, never give out, never give in, keep your faith and you're gonna have a victory."[4]

The story of John Lewis is a profile in courage and bravery in the face of seemingly insurmountable opposition. He is living proof that faith, determination, and commitment to nonviolent direct action can and will change the world. He is still working hard toward his goal of the Beloved Community, but as he has stated many times, it is the young people—passionate, committed students like he once was—who will continue the struggle for true equality in America. Today's battles are different ones from those Lewis fought in his youth, but there are some striking similarities between the civil rights movement and the struggles faced by modern-day Americans of all races, religions, ethnicities, sexual orientations, and gender identities. Lewis won't stop fighting for what's right, and he urges everyone else to find a way to get in the way.

CHRONOLOGY

1940 John Robert Lewis born to Eddie and Willie Mae Lewis on February 21, outside Troy, Alabama.

1954 US Supreme Court rules that segregation in public education is unconstitutional in *Brown v. Board of Education of Topeka*.

1955 Emmett Till is murdered in Money, Mississippi. The Montgomery bus boycott begins when Rosa Parks refuses to give up her seat on a segregated bus.

1957 Lewis enrolls in American Baptist Theological Seminary in Nashville, Tennessee. The Southern Christian Leadership Conference (SCLC) is founded.

1959 Lewis and other Nashville movement students train with James Lawson in his nonviolent direct action workshops.

1960 The Greensboro, North Carolina, sit-ins spark a movement across the South. Lewis and the Nashville students hold a series of sit-ins at lunch counters in downtown department stores. The Student Nonviolent Coordinating Committee (SNCC) is formed.

1961 The Freedom Rides begin in May with Lewis as one of the original thirteen riders.

1963 President John F. Kennedy gives a televised address on civil rights. Lewis is elected chairman of SNCC and becomes one of the Big Six organizers of the March on Washington for Jobs and Freedom, where he gives a speech calling for government action on civil rights. Kennedy is assassinated.

1964 Lewis helps organize and lead the Freedom Summer voter registration campaign in Mississippi. Three Freedom Summer volunteers are murdered. Congress passes the Civil Rights Act of 1964. The Mississippi Freedom Democratic Party (MFDP) unsuccessfully challenges the Mississippi delegation at the Democratic National Convention.

1965 SCLC demonstrations begin in Selma, Alabama. Lewis leads the "Bloody Sunday" march from Selma to Montgomery. President Lyndon B. Johnson signs the Voting Rights Act of 1965.

1966 Lewis loses SNCC chairmanship to Stokely Carmichael and resigns from the organization over ideological differences. Lewis cofounds the Southern Coordinating Committee to End the War in Vietnam and becomes associate director of the Field Foundation.

1967 Lewis graduates from Fisk University and begins work as a community organizer for the Southern Regional Council.

1968 Lewis marries Lillian Miles. He works on Robert (Bobby) Kennedy's presidential campaign until his assassination. Dr. Martin Luther King Jr. is assassinated.

1970 Lewis begins work as executive director of the Voter Education Project.

1975 Lewis wins the Martin Luther King Jr. Peace Prize.

1976 John and Lillian adopt a child, John-Miles Lewis.

1977 Lewis loses his first run for Congress. He is appointed by President Jimmy Carter as director of ACTION.

1981 Lewis is elected to the city council in Atlanta, Georgia.

1986 Lewis is elected to Congress as the US Representative for Georgia's Fifth congressional district.

1988 Lewis is arrested outside of the South African embassy for protesting apartheid-era racial repression.

1991 Lewis opposes Gulf War resolution on the floor of the House.

2006 Lewis is arrested in front of the Sudan embassy for protesting against genocide in Darfur.

2013 Lewis is arrested at a Washington, DC, protest for immigration reform. The US Supreme Court strikes down key provisions of the Voting Rights Act in its *Shelby County v. Holder* decision.

2016 In the wake of a mass shooting in Orlando, Florida, Lewis leads a sit-in on the House floor calling for a vote on gun-control legislation.

2017 Lewis boycotts the inauguration of Donald Trump, who responds by insulting Lewis via Twitter.

GLOSSARY

black nationalism A movement within the civil rights struggle that focused on black pride and advancement, economic self-sufficiency, and black separatism, which stood in contrast to the calls for peaceful integration urged by Dr. Martin Luther King Jr.

border state A former slave state that shared a border with free states to the north.

boycott A concerted effort to get people to stop buying goods and services from a merchant in order to punish that person or to coerce him or her into changing policies.

caste system A set of rigid social categories that determined not only a person's occupation and economic potential, but also his or her position in society.

civil disobedience Opposing a law one considers unjust by peacefully disobeying it and accepting the resultant punishment.

civil rights Constitutional rights and privileges enjoyed by individuals and groups, which the government promises to protect from interference by others.

class action lawsuit A lawsuit brought on behalf of a class of people against a defendant, e.g., a lawsuit brought by those who suffered racial discrimination on a bus line against a person or persons who refused to enforce the law.

commerce clause The clause of the Constitution (Article 1, Section 8, Clause 3) that gives Congress the power to regulate all business activities that cross state lines or affect more than one state or other nations.

conscientious objector An individual who has claimed the right to refuse to perform military service on the grounds of freedom of thought, conscience, and/or religion.

de facto segregation Racial segregation that occurs in schools as a result of patterns of residential settlement, not because of the law.

delegate A person authorized or sent to speak and act for others; a representative, as at a political convention.

disenfranchisement To deprive a person of the right to vote or other rights of citizenship.

double jeopardy The prosecution of a person twice for the same offense.

equal protection clause The portion of the Fourteenth Amendment emphasizing that the laws must provide equivalent protection to all people.

extralegal Something not governed by law or occurring outside the law.

freedom schools A project of the Student Nonviolent Coordinating Committee (SNCC) designed to promote freedom, self-determination, and participatory activism in Mississippi's local black communities and state organizations.

gentrification The process of converting an urban neighborhood from a predominantly low-income, renter-occupied area to a predominantly middle-class, owner-occupied area.

gerrymandering The deliberate rearrangement of the boundaries of congressional districts (especially by racial composition) to influence the outcome of elections.

Jim Crow etiquette A set of social rules that black people had to follow in their everyday lives and interactions with white people.

Jim Crow laws Codified laws enacted by Southern states that discriminated against black people by creating "whites only" schools, bathrooms, drinking fountains, restaurants, bus seating, movie theaters, hotels, and other public accommodations and facilities.

literacy tests Exams implemented by many Southern states as a condition of voting, generally used to disqualify African Americans from voting by imposing impossible and/or arbitrary requirements on black voters but not holding white voters to the same standards.

miscegenation The mixture of races especially marriage, cohabitation, or sexual intercourse between a white person and a member of another race.

pacifism The belief that any violence, including war, is unjustifiable under any circumstances, and that all disputes should be settled by peaceful means.

poll taxes A tax levied in many Southern states that had to be paid before an eligible voter could cast a ballot, aimed at disenfranchising black voters and often due at a time of year when poor African American sharecroppers had the least cash on hand.

prison farm A large, state-run, correctional facility where prisoners are put to economical use in a production capacity, usually for manual labor such as agriculture, logging, quarrying, and mining.

redlining A racially discriminatory practice by which banks, insurance companies, etc., refuse or limit loans, mortgages, insurance, etc., within specific geographic areas, especially inner-city neighborhoods.

separate but equal The doctrine established in *Plessy v. Ferguson* that African Americans could constitutionally be kept in separate but equal facilities.

sharecropping A system of agriculture where a landowner allows a tenant to use the land in return for a share of the crop produced on land. Sharecropping was a widespread response to the economic upheaval caused by the emancipation of slaves and disenfranchisement of poor whites.

sit-ins The act of occupying seats in a racially segregated establishment in organized protest against discrimination.

social gospel The application of Christian principles to social problems faced by people in their earthly lives.

training school Also called vocational school, an institution that prepared students for future employment, especially black students for work as farmers and domestic servants.

white flight The movement of whites out of urban centers to the suburbs.

SOURCES

INTRODUCTION

1. The King Center, "The King Philosophy," KingCenter.org, Accessed September 14, 2018, http://www.thekingcenter.org/king-philosophy.

CHAPTER ONE

1. *Plessy v. Ferguson*, 163 US 537 (1896).

2. John Lewis, *Walking With the Wind: A Memoir of the Movement* (New York: Simon & Schuster, 1998), 47.

3. *Brown v. Board of Education of Topeka*, 347 US 483 (1954).

4. Lewis, *Walking With the Wind*, 48.

CHAPTER TWO

1. Lewis, *Walking With the Wind*, 10.

2. Ibid., 22.

3. Ibid., 36.

4. Ibid., 52.

5. Ibid., 44.

6. Ibid. 45.

7. Ibid., 85.

8. Ibid., 98.

9. Ibid. 100–101.

CHAPTER THREE

1. John F. Kennedy, "Address on Civil Rights" (June 11, 1963), in *The Civil Rights Movement*, written by Peter B. Levy (Westport, CT: Greenwood Press, 1998), 173.

2. Lewis, *Walking With the Wind*, 206.

3. Ibid., 208.

4. Ibid., 204.

5. Ibid. 205.

6. Ibid., 220–221.

CHAPTER FOUR

1. Lewis, *Walking With the Wind*, 129.

2. Ibid., 143–144.

3. Ibid., 249.

4. Fannie Lou Hamer, "Testimony Before the Credentials Committee, Democratic National Convention, Atlantic City, New Jersey, August 22, 1964," in *The Speeches of Fannie Lou Hamer: To Tell It Like It Is*, edited by Maegan Parker Brooks and Davis W. Houck (Jackson, MS: University Press of Mississippi, 2011), 44.

5. Lyndon B. Johnson, "Special Message to the Congress: The American Promise" (March 15, 1965), in *The Civil Rights Movement*, written by Peter B. Levy (Westport, CT: Greenwood Press, 1998), 183–184.

6. *Voting Rights Act of 1965*, Public Law 89-110, *US Statutes at Large* 79 (1965): 437.

CHAPTER FIVE

1. *Civil Rights Act of 1964*, Public Law 88-352, *US Statutes at Large* 78 (1964): 241.

2. Lewis, *Walking With the Wind*, 118.

3. John Lewis, "Interview with John Lewis," Interview by Janet Heininger, *The Miller Center: Edward M. Kennedy Oral History Project*, December 4, 2006: 4.

4. Lewis, *Walking With the Wind*, 413.

5. Ibid., 399.

6. Ibid., 447.

CHAPTER SIX

1. John Lewis, with Brenda Jones. *Across That Bridge: A Vision for Change and the Future of America* (New York: Hachette Books, 2017): 187.

2. Lewis, John, "Rep. John Lewis Calls Court Decision 'A Dagger' In the Heart of Voting Access," June 25, 2013. https://johnlewis.house.gov/media-center/press-releases/rep-john-lewis-calls-court-decision-dagger-heart-voting-access.

3. Lewis, John, "At a Crossroads on Gay Unions," *The Boston Globe*, October 25, 2003. http://archive.boston.com/news/globe/editorial_opinion/oped/articles/2003/10/25/at_a_crossroads_on_gay_unions.

4. 11Alive. "'Don't Give Up' Congressman John Lewis Speaks At Atlanta March For Our Lives Rally." Filmed March 24, 2018. YouTube video. 5:56. Posted March 24, 2018. https://www.youtube.com/watch?v=0vOaIHI0nBk.

FURTHER INFORMATION

BOOKS

Boehme, Gerry. *Primary Sources of the Civil Rights Movement: John Lewis and Desegregation*. New York: Cavendish Square, 2017.

Lewis, John, with Brenda Jones. *Across That Bridge: A Vision for Change and the Future of America.* New York: Hachette Books, 2017.

Long, Michael, ed. *We the Resistance: Documenting a History of Nonviolent Protest in the United States*. San Francisco, CA: City Lights Publishers, 2019.

Pratt, Robert A. *Selma's Bloody Sunday: Protest, Voting Rights, and the Struggle for Racial Equality*. Baltimore, MD: The Johns Hopkins University Press, 2017.

WEBSITES

The Black Past: Remembered and Reclaimed
https://blackpast.org

This online reference center focuses on African American history and the African diaspora, with over fifteen thousand encyclopedia entries, as well as images, primary source documents, and timelines.

Congressman John Lewis
https://johnlewis.house.gov

This is the official website for Congressman John Lewis, which includes his positions on major issues, recent voting records, and press releases.

Digital History
http://www.digitalhistory.uh.edu

This comprehensive multimedia reference site covers American history by both time period and topics, which includes primary source documents, images, timelines, glossaries, and maps.

MUSEUMS AND ORGANIZATIONS

Birmingham Civil Rights Institute
520 16th Street N
Birmingham, Alabama 35203

The National Civil Rights Museum
450 Mulberry Street
Memphis, Tennessee 38103

The National Museum of African American History and Culture
1400 Constitution Avenue NW
Washington, DC 20560

BIBLIOGRAPHY

Anderson, Elizabeth, and Jeffrey Jones. "The Geography of Race in the United States." University of Michigan. Accessed September 23, 2018. http://umich.edu/~lawrace.

Bash, Dana. "Following John Lewis on Civil Rights Journey Touched by the Spirit of History." CNN.com. March 9, 2018. https://www.cnn.com/2018/03/07/politics/john-lewis-bloody-sunday-anniversary-reporters-notebook/index.html.

Berman, Ari. *Give Us the Ballot: The Modern Struggle for Voting Rights in America.* New York: Picador, 2016.

Boehme, Gerry. *John Lewis and Desegregation.* New York: Cavendish Square, 2017.

Branch, Taylor. *Parting the Waters: America in the King Years, 1954-63.* New York: Simon & Schuster, 1988.

———. *Pillar of Fire: America in the King Years, 1963–65.* New York: Simon & Schuster, 1998.

———. *At Canaan's Edge: America in the King Years, 1965–1968.* New York: Simon & Schuster, 2006.

Brooks, Maegan Parker, and Davis W. Houck, eds. *The Speeches of Fannie Lou Hamer: To Tell It Like It Is.* Jackson: University Press of Mississippi, 2011.

Cagin, Seth, and Philip Dray. *We Are Not Afraid: The Story of Goodman, Schwerner, and Chaney and the Civil Rights Campaign for Mississippi*. New York: Bantam, 1991.

Carson, Clayborne. *In Struggle: SNCC and the Black Awakening of the 1960s*. Cambridge, MA: Harvard University Press, 1981.

Carson, Clayborne, David J. Garrow, Gerald Gill, Vincent Harding, and Darlene Clark Hine, eds. *The Eyes on the Prize Civil Rights Reader*. New York: Penguin Books, 1991.

Hendrick, George, and Willene Hendrick. *Why Not Every Man?: African Americans and Civil Disobedience in the Quest for the Dream*. Chicago: Ivan R. Dee, 2005.

Hill, Christine M. *John Lewis: From Freedom Rider to Congressman*. Berkeley Heights, NJ: Enslow Publishers, 2002.

Hogan, Wesley C. *Many Minds, One Heart: SNCC's Dream for a New America*. Durham, NC: The University of North Carolina Press, 2009.

John Lewis: Get in the Way. Directed by Kathleen Dowdey. 2017. Public Broadcasting Service (PBS). DVD.

The King Center, "The King Philosophy," KingCenter.org. Accessed September 14, 2018. http://www.thekingcenter. org/king-philosophy.

Levy, Peter B. *The Civil Rights Movement.* Westport, CT: Greenwood Press, 1998.

Lewis, John. "At A Crossroads on Gay Unions." *Boston Globe.* October 25, 2003. http://archive.boston.com/news/ globe/editorial_opinion/oped/articles/2003/10/25/at_a_ crossroads_on_gay_unions.

———. "Interview with John Lewis." Interview by Janet Heininger. *The Miller Center: Edward M. Kennedy Oral History Project.* December 4, 2006. Accessed September 5, 2018. http://web1.millercenter.org/poh/transcripts/ ohp_2006_1204_lewis.pdf.

———. "Speech at the March on Washington." *Voices Of Democracy: The US Oratory Project.* Accessed October 1, 2018. http://voicesofdemocracy.umd.edu/lewis-speech-at-the-march-on-washington-textual-authentication.

———. "Rep. John Lewis Calls Court Decision 'A Dagger' In the Heart of Voting Access." JohnLewis.House.Gov. June 25, 2013. https://johnlewis.house.gov/media-center/ press-releases/rep-john-lewis-calls-court-decision-dagger-heart-voting-access.

Lewis, John, and Andrew Aydin. *March: Book One.* Marietta, GA: Top Shelf Productions, 2013.

———. *March: Book Two.* Marietta, GA: Top Shelf Productions, 2015.

———. *March: Book Three.* Marietta, GA: Top Shelf Productions, 2016.

Lewis, John, with Brenda Jones. *Across That Bridge: A Vision for Change and the Future of America.* New York: Hachette Books, 2017.

Lewis, John, with Michael D'Orso. *Walking With the Wind: A Memoir of the Movement.* New York: Simon & Schuster, 1998.

Morgan, Iwan, and Philip Davies, Eds. *From Sit-Ins to SNCC: The Student Civil Rights Movement in the 1960s.* Gainesville, FL: The University Press of Florida, 2013.

Morretta, Alison. *Primary Sources of the Civil Rights Movement: Rosa Parks and Civil Disobedience.* New York: Cavendish Square, 2017.

Morris, Aldon D. *The Origins of the Civil Rights Movement: Black Communities Organizing for Change.* New York: The Free Press, 1984.

Nicols, John. "Demanding Votes on Gun-Control Bills, John Lewis Leads a Sit-in of the House." *Nation.* June 22, 2016. https://www.thenation.com/article/demanding-votes-on-gun-control-bills-john-lewis-leads-a-sit-in-of-the-house.

On the Issues. "John Lewis on Civil Rights." OnTheIssues.org. Accessed September 10, 2018. http://www.ontheissues.org/GA/John_Lewis_Civil_Rights.htm.

Pazzanese, Christina, "John Lewis Urges: Back 'the Beloved Community.'" *Harvard Gazette.* April 17, 2017. https://news.harvard.edu/gazette/story/2017/04/civil-rights-icon-john-lewis-headed-to-harvard-sees-work-ahead-to-guarantee-rights.

Pérez-Peña, Richard. "Woman Linked to 1955 Emmett Till Murder Tells Historian Her Claims Were False." *New York Times.* January 27, 2017. https://www.nytimes.com/2017/01/27/us/emmett-till-lynching-carolyn-bryant-donham.html.

Tyson, Timothy B. *The Blood of Emmett Till.* New York: Simon & Schuster, 2017.

Rafferty, Andrew. "Democratic Lawmakers Arrested During Immigration Protest." NBC News.com. October 8, 2013. https://www.nbcnews.com/politics/politics-news/democratic-lawmakers-arrested-during-immigration-protest-flna8C11360069.

Williams, Juan. *Eyes on the Prize: America's Civil Rights Years, 1954–1965.* New York: Viking, 1987.

INDEX

equal protection clause, 10
extralegal, 22–23

faith, 5–6, 26, 105
Farmer, James, 49, 51–52, 60–61, 64
Fellowship of Reconciliation (FOR), 35–36
Fifteenth Amendment, 10, 22
Fisk University, 37, 68, 88
Fourteenth Amendment, 10, 20
freedom clinics, 69
Freedom Rides, 47, 51, 59–60, **62**, **66**, 67, 84
freedom schools, 69, 72–73

gentrification, 91
gerrymandering, 97
graphic novels, 102–103, **103**
Gray, Fred, 35
gun-control legislation, 104–105, **105**

Hamer, Fannie Lou, 74–75

immigration, **7**, 43, 96, 101

Jim Crow etiquette, 12, 17
Jim Crow laws, 10–12, 17
Johnson, President Lyndon B., 69, 72, 74, 78–79, 82–84, 86

Kennedy, President John F., 48–50, **49**, 52–53, 64–65, 68, 82, 84, 104
Kennedy, Robert F. "Bobby", 65, 81, 84, **85**, 86–88, 104
Kennedy administration, 47, 49, 51–54, 64
King, Martin Luther, Jr., 6, 19–20, **21**, 22, 33–35, 41, **44**, 46, 49–51, **49**, 53–54, 66, 74, 76, 78, **81**, 86–88, 102, 104
Ku Klux Klan, 20, 23, 63

Lawson, Reverend James, 35–38, **36**, 40, 46–47, 68
Lewis, Lillian, **87**, 88, 92
Lewis, Willie Mae, 25, 31
LGBTQ rights, 7, 98, **99**, 100
literacy tests, 22, 76, 82
Little Rock Nine, 34, **34**
lynching, 13–14

March on Washington for Jobs and Freedom, 49–50, 53–54, **55**, **81**, 86
martial law, 66
miscegenation, 12
Mississippi Freedom Democratic Party (MFDP), 73–75
Mississippi Freedom Summer, 53, 59, **70**

Montgomery bus boycott, 16, **18**, 22, 35, 46

Nash, Diane, 38, 40, 46–47, 64
Nashville, Tennessee, 6, 36–40, 46–47, 53, 64, 67–68, 77
National Association for the Advancement of Colored People (NAACP), 17, 19–20, 33–34, 49, 51, 68
National Guard, 48, 66, 79
National Urban League, 49, 51
Nineteenth Amendment, 22

pacifism, 36
Parks, Rosa, 18–20, 35
Plessy v. Ferguson, 10–11, 17
poll taxes, 22, 82
prison farm, 67

Randolph, A. Philip, 49–51, 53–54
redlining, 92
Robinson, Jo Ann, 18–19

segregation, 11, 17, 20, 36, 38, 47–48, 50, 60, 82, 92
Selma, Alabama, 7, 59, 74, 76–79, **77**, 82, 102
seminary, 6, 33
separate but equal, 11, 17
sharecropping, **24**, 25–26

Shelby County v. Holder, 97–98
sit-ins, 7, 36, 38–41, **42**, 43, 46, 52, 61, 74, 101, 104
social gospel, 6, 33, 37
social justice, 6, 22, 33, 46, 88
Southern Christian Leadership Conference (SCLC), 45–46, 49–50, 60, 68, 76–78, 90
Student Nonviolent Coordinating Committee (SNCC), 36, 45–49, 51–54, 56, 60, 64, 68–71, 74–78, 82, 88–90

Till, Emmett, 14–16, **14**
training school, 32
Troy, Alabama, 25, 31, 34–35

United States Supreme Court, 10, 16–17, 20, 60, 83, 97, 100

voter registration, 6, 22–23, 47, 53, 68–69, 73, 76, 82, 90
voter suppression, 17, 68–69, 83, 98
Voting Rights Act of 1965, 79, 82, **83**, 97–98

white flight, 92
Wilkins, Roy, 49, 51, 54, 74

ABOUT THE AUTHOR

Alison Morretta holds a bachelor of arts in English and creative writing from Kenyon College in Gambier, Ohio, where she studied literature and American history. She has written many nonfiction titles for middle and high school students on subjects such as American literature, the abolitionist movement, the civil rights era, westward expansion, internet safety, and Islamophobia. She lives in New York City with her loving husband, Bart, and their rambunctious Corgi, Cassidy.